UPON IMPACT

*Two Women's Journeys through Friendship,
Tragedy, and Love*

Stacy A Buehner

ISBN: 1511705108
ISBN 13: 978-1511705103
Library of Congress Control Number: 2015906436
CreateSpace Independent Publishing Platform
North Charleston, South Carolina

For Kristy, my soul sister

ACKNOWLEDGMENTS

Thank you to my friends and family for your love and support. A special thank you to my husband for your love and devotion. Deep gratitude to the ladies of Brookings Masters of Minds for your support and encouragement. You have all impacted my life in more ways than you can imagine.

Many names of the characters in this story have been changed to protect their privacy.

CHAPTER 1
THE CAR ACCIDENT

It was a hot, sunny day, July 3, 2001, when my best friend, Kristy, and I were driving down Highway 81 in South Dakota. We were on our way home from a week-long trip to Minneapolis. I was in the passenger seat of Kristy's gray 1985 Astro minivan. It looked like one of those vans drug dealers use—rusted, beat-up, with no air conditioning and no backseat. Since it was almost ninety degrees outside, I was wearing my yellow bikini top and shorts. It truly was a beautiful day. I looked out my passenger window, taking in the vibrant green cornfields with the warm wind blowing on my face. It was a day that I would remember for the rest of my life.

Out of nowhere, Kristy screamed, "Oh no!" I instantly turned my head and caught a glimpse of a green tractor loader coming right at us. I looked at Kristy to make sure she saw what was about to happen. She turned the wheel in an attempt to swerve around the loader.

I knew we were going to hit the ditch going seventy miles per hour (highways in South Dakota have a speed limit of sixty-five). I closed my eyes and gripped my seat belt. Thank God I was wearing it. *Thank God.*

I felt the shattering glass hit and pierce my face. I clutched my face with my hands and started to scream. I could hear the van's metal structure rip and crunch.

After rolling two and a half times, the van landed on its right side. I removed my hands from my face—blood was all over them. I was hanging by my seat belt, tilting to the right. My window was now facing the ground. The seat belt was digging into my stomach, and I hurt all over. I unbuckled my seat belt and fell inside the van. I was distraught and confused. I thought I was dreaming. *Wake up, Stacy. Wake up!* I yelled at myself. Fear and panic started to set in. *Kristy! Where is Kristy?* I looked up above me at her seat. She wasn't there. I looked into the back of the van. She wasn't there either. I tried to look outside. I couldn't see her. *Cell phone. Where is my mom's cell phone?* I started to cry and yell for help. I was trapped in the van, glass was all around me, and I was bleeding. I could smell the dirty oil dripping from the engine. It was nauseating. I couldn't find my purse with my mom's cell phone. The situation was hopeless.

Then I heard a voice. I peeked out through the twisted metal and saw a boy who looked to be about twelve years old, with bright blond hair and a stocky build. He looked like my little brother. He was crying and looked utterly terrified; he was the one driving the tractor that hit us. He asked me if I was okay. I told him I needed help and that he should call 911. I asked him if he was by himself. He seemed too young to be driving the tractor alone. He was indeed. The big sister in me started to kick in. *Stop crying—you need to take control. You are the adult here.* I was nineteen. I asked him where Kristy was. Shaking, he pointed off to the right. I still couldn't see her. I knew it wasn't good—Kristy had been thrown from the van.

The boy went to his house, which was right across the highway, to get help. Then a young woman, probably in her midtwenties, suddenly appeared right outside the van. She grabbed my hand and asked if I was okay. She said she was in training to be a nurse. I started to cry again. I told her that I couldn't find Kristy and asked if she was okay. She didn't answer but started to rub my legs in an effort to keep my blood flowing and to prevent me from going into shock. She assured me that I was going to be okay. My toes were in excruciating pain. I looked down at them. I had a long cut all across my toes, from my pinky toe and ending before my big toe. The middle toe next to the pinky hurt the worst, and I couldn't really move it. *Well, if my grandpa can do okay with a missing thumb, I should be okay with one less toe. Hmm…although it would be hard to wear sandals in summer—I'd look pretty funny.* I told myself that if all I lost was a toe, I'd be lucky.

Minutes passed, and then the paramedics came. Chaos started to happen. People were running around. "Shoot! I just moved her head!" one paramedic yelled.

I thought to myself, *Well, if I'm going to be paralyzed, I've done it to myself already, since I've been moving around.* It was clear that the rural paramedics had never seen such a horrible sight. I think I told them my parents' phone number about a hundred million times. They began to ask me questions: "Do you know what day it is?"

"July third," I said.

"Who is the president?"

I replied, "Bush."

They asked me if I had been at the beach that day (because I was wearing my bikini top). Funny. I wish I had been at the beach at that very moment. They didn't know how to get me out of the van. "We need to use the Jaws of Life to get her out," said another paramedic. They put a blanket over me and started to drill and cut into the van to get me out.

Why don't they just take me out through the back of the van? I thought. The drilling stopped. A paramedic came back inside the van to me. "We are going to take you out the back." *Good, finally they are using their heads.*

They put a neck support on me and placed me on a stretcher. I could hear a helicopter. When they loaded me into it, I looked around. *Where is Kristy? She must need to go to the hospital too.* I told myself that they must have sent another helicopter for her. The new paramedics put an oxygen mask on me and started to ask me questions. What a pain; it was like being at the dentist when they start interrogating you. Like you can really talk? Despite the fact that the paramedics were taking very good care of me, the helicopter ride was extremely uncomfortable.

Once in the emergency room in Sioux Falls, things started to happen fast. There were nurses (mostly good-looking men) running around and getting things for Dr. Harris, a large, burly man with white hair and a white mustache who looked like Santa Claus. One of the female nurses told me that I was in luck because Dr. Harris, the best stitching surgeon, was working to-night—so I would have very few scars. I began to think about my boyfriend, because I had told him that I would call him when I got home. Then I remembered that his dad was a well-known dermatologist and worked at this hospital. I told the nurses to call Dr. Smith. They looked very confused.

"You have to tell Dr. Smith in dermatology that I am here," I told them again.

"He's not in right now; he's at home," one of the nurses told me, still looking very confused.

Then I told her that his son was my boyfriend.

"Oh, okay," she said.

They finally understood why I was demanding they talk to Dr. Smith, but of course they didn't call him.

"Were you wearing a seat belt?" asked Dr. Harris.

"Yes," I replied.

"Do you smoke?" he asked.

"No," I replied.

"Good girl!" he said in his scratchy voice.

One of the cute male nurses started to clean the cuts on my toes and then stitched the deep cut.

"You are very lucky—you almost lost this toe," he said.

Dr. Harris started to clean the cut on my eyebrow. This was all happening while another nurse tried to take blood from my arm and another nurse stuck an IV in each of my wrists. The pain was unbearable. I'm a tough girl, but that was too much. They gave me morphine.

After a while, Dr. Harris and I were the only ones left in the room. He was stitching up the cut to my eyebrow. I stayed strong and didn't cry so that he could do his job well. Then a nurse came in and told me my mom was outside. They were going to let her come in after they cleaned me up.

"I bet my mom is freaking out," I told them.

I was very much still in shock and had been making jokes with everybody in the emergency room.

My mom walked in the room, crying. Behind her was a man I had never seen before, a priest from the hospital.

"I'm okay, Mom! I didn't break any bones!" I said enthusiastically.

She hugged me, and I began to try to tell her what happened.

"A tractor hit us, Mom. This boy, this little boy...he was probably fourteen years old or something, hit us... He came out of nowhere...All I saw was this tractor coming at us...He was just a little kid," I said.

I asked her what happened to Kristy.

She looked deep into my eyes. "She's gone, honey. She didn't make it," my mom sobbed.

I had known deep down that she was dead, but hearing my mom say it out loud made it real. I cried for a while and then stopped. My mom told me we would get me therapy. She was scared I'd lose it after having my best friend die. I asked her to call my boyfriend's parents. She used the phone in the emergency room to make the call. His parents were very concerned and shocked—of course. They came to see me later, along with the rest of my family.

That night, the nurses put cuff-like things on my legs and a blood pressure device on my arm. The cuff-like things would expand and tighten all night. My mom stayed with me the entire night, sleeping in the chair in front of my bed. The IVs were the worst things I had ever experienced, these horrible, large, long, painful, cold metal needles stuck in both of my wrists. I could feel them inside my wrists and so badly wanted to rip them out.

I thought about how horrible it would be not to have Kristy in my life anymore. I had a sickening, empty feeling in my heart. I knew that I was in shock and that eventually I would have to grieve. It would be a long, sad, horrible process. I told myself that for right now, I needed to focus on getting better.

When morning came, I felt like I'd been hit by a truck. The expression that I had heard many times before had a new meaning to me. *Ha-ha*, I told myself. *Oh no, you were hit by a tractor!* One of the nurses took me out of my bed and walked with me around the floor. I was very weak. I was put in a wheelchair and taken out to my mom's car. I felt so lucky that I hadn't lost my legs. It was a very bittersweet feeling, being so thankful that I was alive, intertwined with the deep sadness of losing my best friend forever.

No one tells you that the tragic, difficult times in your life will shape you into who you become, or that those times will change you forever. It's how we deal with these difficult times and what we learn from them that truly makes a difference.

Some people turn to God or a higher being, while others turn to drugs or alcohol. Some take it out on others, and some are able to do something positive. Others retreat and hold it inside. No matter how you deal with your life's challenges, the key is that you have gone through this difficult situation to become a better person. You hold the power to take from it what you will, and hopefully, you turn it into something positive or it gives you a new outlook on life.

The saying "Life is short" is common; "short" can mean different things to different people. It could be a few hours, days, months, or years. When someone dies in her eighties or nineties, we say that she lived a long life. My best friend lived until the age of nineteen, yet she could have been eighty-five with all that she had gone through. Sometimes I think those who push the limits and take the greatest risks often die young. They jam-pack everything into a few short years. I suppose it really lies in what God has planned for you.

CHAPTER 2
THE EARLY YEARS

Kristy and I went way back. We had been friends since kindergarten. Her family moved into a house in the country about two miles from mine. They had come from Montana to just outside a small rural town in South Dakota. We used to ride our bikes down the gravel road to meet each other halfway. Life was simple then. We both came from good, strong families, though Kristy was always getting into trouble, not because she was rebellious but because she was just so darn curious. She had a true zest for life. Kristy wasn't afraid of anything or anyone. She went along her way, minding her own business, walking to the beat of her own drum.

"I don't get into trouble; it just finds me," she would always say with a laugh. "You shouldn't worry so much, Stacy. You need to go with the flow." I was always the one to keep her on track; she was always pushing the limits too far. I was the solid, reasonable, common-sense half of our friendship. Physically, she was just a little taller, but we both had blue eyes and brown hair (unless we had it colored). Kristy dressed in a simple, classy way, but always a little flashy to get some attention whenever she could.

Kristy and I didn't always get along; we were both stubbornly independent, even as kids. Like her mother, Kristy was outspoken. This didn't get her the popular card, so for quite a few years, we weren't close friends. We were both in Girl Scouts one year, and after school we would ride the bus to our troop leader's house. There were about five girls who joined. One evening on the school bus on our way to the meeting, Kristy and I had a falling-out. I was sitting between two other girls, Sam and Nikki. Kristy was sitting across the aisle in the other seat. Kristy and I had been fighting all day. She offered Sam and Nikki a piece of gum but didn't offer any to me. Knowing that Kristy was trying to make me upset, Nikki gave me half of her piece. I stuck it in my mouth, faced Kristy, and started chewing loudly so that she would see that I had gotten some, even though she didn't want me to have any. The next thing I knew, Kristy's fist was headed right for my nose. Yep, she punched me square in the nose. It hurt, but I wasn't bleeding, although to this day I claim that her punching me is why I have a slightly crooked nose!

Kristy had a younger brother, Brent. He was a little spitfire. Sometimes when he would get excited, his eyes would bug out and he would skip words when he was talking. Since Kristy had Brent and I had an older brother, the four of us would hang out a lot during the summer. We made forts out of junk and played girls-versus-boys games. We even had a fort in my grandparents' barn. We cleaned it out, decorated it, and hauled old furniture into it. It was awesome.

One summer day, Kristy and Brent came over to my house. She got the idea that we should go "fishing" for crawfish in our creek. She brought over a minnow bucket, and we headed for the creek. My brother Troy, Kristy, and Brent went down into the creek and started to grab the crawfish. I stayed above on the bridge and watched them down below. No way was I going to touch those things. After they caught about five crawfish, we brought them inside the house to cook them. Kristy said she knew exactly how to cook them. She grabbed a big pot, put the crawfish in there, and started to boil the water. She covered the pot with a lid and continued to bat at the crawfish to keep them in there. I was grossed out, not too happy that we were cooking live fish. Then, once Kristy was convinced that the crawfish were cooked, she made Brent and Troy try one. Well, I don't recall how much they ate, but I wasn't going to touch them. Kristy put the leftover crawfish in the freezer. A few hours later, my mom came home from work.

"Hmm...what should we make for dinner?" she mumbled.

Then she opened the freezer. "Oh my gosh, what is this?" she asked me as she pulled out the bag of crawfish.

"Oh, those are the crawfish that Kristy cooked. Troy and Brent ate one," I said nonchalantly.

My mom got quiet and gave me her serious look. "Stacy, don't ever do that again."

When we were in the fourth grade, boys stopped having cooties, although for me, they never had. I had a longtime crush on one our neighbors, Austin. His parents were good friends with mine, so I saw him often. Whenever we saw each other, he would start to flirt with me (well, the way a second grader flirts). He gave me my first kiss. After a while, our parents got busy, so they saw less of each other, meaning that Austin and I saw less of each other too (we also didn't attend the same school). But I told myself that it was okay, and that he was too much of a cowboy for me. Then, around fifth grade, Kristy started hanging out with Austin. Because Kristy and I were good friends, she asked me if it would be all right if she and Austin started to date. I told her it was completely fine (I had him first anyway). After all, Kristy and I had very different tastes in men. And Austin really was too much of a cowboy for me; I don't wear Wranglers and ride horses.

Kristy fell pretty hard for Austin, who was your classic Casanova. By the time we were sixteen, that boy had already slept with a handful of women. I guess he had a certain rustic charm about him.

Kristy's dad, James, was a take-charge, authoritative, smug man with a loud, booming voice and a great sense of humor. Her mom, Emily, didn't seem like the type of woman who would stay with Kristy's dad. Emily was opinionated, strong, and very outspoken. I never understood how the two of them stayed married. They didn't even sleep in the same room. Emily would sleep in the bedroom, and James would sleep on the couch in the living room. James claimed he slept on the couch because he had a bad back.

Emily worked as a travel agent and was a very good one at that. She often stood up to her boss and continued to get pay raises and gifts. James had moved to South Dakota to become a hog farmer. At that time, there was money to be made in that business. They also had plenty of horses, chickens, cows, dogs, and cats. Kristy loved pigs; she would tell people that pigs are a lot cleaner than most people think. She would refer to them as "cute." Kristy was more obsessed with pigs than anything. She had stuffed animal pigs all over her room and pig figurines all over the house. I liked pigs, too, but only because they were pink.

The summer before sixth grade, Kristy's dad decided they should move back to Bozeman, Montana (from where they had originally come). Once James decided, it was done. End of discussion. I'm not sure if that was a long time coming, a thoughtful decision, or if James woke up one day and decided on it. He was the man of the house, and what he wanted and what he said was what the family had to follow. Perhaps he wasn't making enough money as a hog farmer, or perhaps he just wanted to move back to where his heart truly was.

I'm not sure if this was a happy decision on his part, because the night before they moved, James got drunk and trashed the farm. There was broken glass all over, beer cans thrown about, and doors had been broken— it was as if he had a breakdown.

The day Kristy's family moved back to Montana, we said our good-byes. We told each other that we would stay in touch and write letters often.

CHAPTER 3

AFTER THE MOVE

As we promised, Kristy and I stayed in touch. What I didn't know was that we would become best friends, even though we were 825 miles apart.

Every chance we got, we would try to see each other. My uncle Brad lived near Seattle and would often drive out to South Dakota during the summer. When he drove back to Seattle, I would catch a ride with him since he drove through Bozeman. Brad owned a jewelry store in Snohomish, a small, quaint town near Seattle. He was a businessman at heart who felt that no one could run his store but him. He also did a lot of old-fashioned bartering. For example, he was friends with a man who owned a cruise company, so my uncle might give his friend some exquisite diamond earrings, and in return, my aunt and uncle would go on a Caribbean cruise for their anniversary—not a bad deal, if you ask me.

When I was fifteen, my parents decided I was old enough to visit Kristy, so I rode with my aunt and uncle in their sporty silver BMW (and yes, Uncle Brad was also friends with a car dealer). Needless to say, after that trip, I had a strong affection for BMWs.

Kristy often talked about their "ranch" near Ennis, Montana. Based on that, I expected to see an extravagant house with huge fenced areas and lots of horses. Their "ranch" house was more like a small cabin. Her dad was working for a man who owned a couple of large, successful ranches. I distinctly remember James driving a large white pickup truck, single cab only, with a wooden flatbed as the back. He was a typical rancher, wearing glasses, a cowboy hat, Wranglers, and cowboy boots on a daily basis. He loved his kids and his family, and he loved Montana. James always had a sense of pride in being from that state.

Kristy had a part-time job at a small motel nearby. She cleaned the rooms, not a fun job by any means, but not dull either. It was summertime, and in the mountains there were a lot of young men logging. For those of you who don't know what loggers are, they used to be called lumberjacks. Apparently it is a great-paying job.

One day during my visit, Kristy suggested I join her as she cleaned rooms. In one of the rooms there were two guys older than us (we were both fifteen). One guy was nineteen and the other was twenty-two. They had a *Playboy* magazine in the bathroom, condoms, cigarettes, and clothes thrown about. *Messy boys.* Kristy got this crazy idea that we should write them a note. She started the letter by saying that we were both seventeen. (She didn't want to say we were over eighteen; that way they couldn't do anything illegal with us.) Then she told them that if they were interested, they should call us. She left them her parents' home number. Surprise, surprise, the guys called. Kristy told me that her dad was a logger when he was younger and that he would not be happy to know that we were going on a date with two loggers. So we kept it secret. We snuck out of her parents' house, telling them we were going to a movie in a nearby town. I was really nervous. This was my first date, and I was lying about my age! Kristy thought it was no big deal.

The two guys drove a beat-up, rusty, dirty old seventies Chevy Suburban. Mike, the nineteen-year-old, was tall and lanky, with dirty-blond hair and glasses. Not my type at all. The twenty-two-year-old, Darrell, was tall, muscular, dark, and handsome—much more my type. So Kristy and I agreed that Darrell was mine, and she would get Mike.

The night started out pretty normal. We went to dinner at a local restaurant and then for a drive to look at the stars. Afterward, we went to a local bar. Of course,

Kristy and I didn't drink. Kristy and Mike started to play darts, while Darrell and I hung out at the bar. Darrell started to put the moves on me. He put his hand on my leg and started to whisper in my ear. Well, I wasn't about to do anything with him. In fact, the way I was dressed should have given him a clue. I was wearing a short-sleeved dark-blue turtleneck (even though it was the middle of summer) and a necklace with a cross. Then Darrell suggested to Kristy and me that we should go back to their place. Kristy responded by saying, "I'm not that kind of girl." Thank goodness, because I wasn't sure what I would have done had she said something different!

The evening was fun for two fifteen-year-old boy-crazy girls. A couple of days later we decided to see the guys again. So we drove to the motel, which was only a about a mile away. We decided to play a card game (we weren't doing anything bad). The next thing we knew, we heard Kristy's dad come barreling into the motel parking area in his truck, speeding up to the room where Kristy's Jeep was parked. A cloud of dust was flying as he flew into the parking lot. He was honking the horn and yelling at us.

"*Kristy*, get out here, now! Girls, you are going home, *now!*"

Boy, was he mad! Somehow he had found out about the boys. I suspect that someone from the motel called him when they saw Kristy's Jeep parked by the boys' room. I guess James remembered what it was like when he was a young logger, and he knew exactly what the guys were after.

That pretty much ended our fun with them. So Kristy and I had to find other things to stay occupied. Kristy decided that she would show me around the area. We went hiking in the mountains, taking a shotgun with us because of the bears. Kristy decided to show me some of the other mountains in the area, driving her mom's Jeep Jimmy. We were attempting to drive up a very steep hill, but I don't think Kristy sped up enough to make it. So she decided to go in reverse to try again. But when the Jeep was put in reverse, the brakes stopped working. Kristy frantically continued to hit the brakes, but nothing was happening. We began to pick up more speed, flying backward down the gravel road. The Jeep went into the ditch and kept going until it hit a huge wooden post in the driveway of someone's ranch. I heard a crash and then the sound of glass breaking. I sat there, shocked. Kristy was freaking out. She jumped out of the Jeep and started crying. I turned off the radio and got out too. The back windshield was smashed and there was a dent in the bumper. Kristy and I went up the driveway to the house. The woman who lived there was very calm and had us call Kristy's mom. Emily and James came and picked us up. Emily wasn't happy, but she was glad that we weren't hurt. I thought for sure they were going to send me home that night.

Emily and James were having marital problems. Emily had been spending a lot of time with one of her female coworkers who was battling cancer. Sometimes she would bring her coworker's dog home with her, and we would take care of the dog. It seemed as if James was angry that Emily was spending so much time with her cancer-stricken friend. Perhaps James's pride was getting in the way. He wanted to be the center of Emily's attention. Or maybe they had been having marital issues for a long time. When they were living in South Dakota, they didn't even sleep in the same room. But being a fifth grader doesn't make you an expert on marriage, nor do you really understand or notice red flags between married people. Now, in my thirties, I can spot those red flags, but I have also gained the knowledge that every couple is different, and every couple has their quirks and different ways of keeping their relationship strong. I can also spot couples who are struggling.

While I was staying with Kristy and her family, I awoke early in the morning and overheard Emily and James talking in the kitchen. I didn't see them but envisioned them sitting at the kitchen table talking over a cup of coffee. I only heard bits and pieces of their conversation:

"So what should we do?" Emily asked. "What are we going to do with the kids?"

I couldn't make out what James was saying. I didn't say anything to Kristy about what I heard because I didn't want her to worry in case I misunderstood what I had heard. But I was concerned.

My cousin, Toni, and her husband were in Montana visiting some friends, so I took a bus to meet her so that I could ride back to South Dakota with them. As I got on the bus, I hugged Kristy, Brent, Emily, and James and said good-bye. I didn't know that it was the last time I would see Emily alive.

CHAPTER 4
FAMILY SECRETS

After I left that summer, I have no idea what happened between Emily and James. My focus changed to my own family. My uncle Steve was fighting throat cancer, and my family was dealing with other difficult issues.

October 1997 was one of the worst months of my life. Uncle Steve lost his battle with throat cancer. I had watched him deteriorate in the hospital. The only way he could speak was through a specialized vibration tool held up to his voice box. My mom visited him every day. It was very difficult to watch my mom grieve for her older brother. I had never seen her cry so much. On the day of his funeral, my family gathered at my uncle's bar; we made a toast with Jack Daniel's, which was his favorite drink. My family told me I had to take a shot with them in honor of my uncle. As I took the shot, I made a promise to myself that I wouldn't ever drink or smoke. Uncle Steve had been an alcoholic and a heavy smoker. I didn't want to end up like him. He was a brilliant lawyer, but his personal choices—and alcoholism—made him go down a road that ended his life at the early age of fifty-six.

A week or so after my uncle's death, Emily was on her way to Kristy and Brent's concert at school. She never made it there. During her drive to the school, a young man wasn't paying attention, swerved into oncoming traffic, and hit Emily's vehicle head-on. She died on impact.

The events that followed opened up a world of family secrets.

I will never forget Kristy's phone call late in the evening. She could hardly get the words out. "Stacy, something horrible has happened," she sobbed. "My mom died! She was in a car accident, and she's dead."

I couldn't believe it. I was in complete shock and had no idea what to say. So I just tried to comfort her as best I could.

"I'm so sorry, Kristy. I'm here for you—whatever you need," I told her. "Listen, it's late; try to get some sleep, and I'll call you tomorrow. Hang in there. It will be all right."

Her world was crashing down, spinning out of control, and there was nothing she could do about it.

Kristy told me I didn't need to go to the funeral—and the fact that I was in South Dakota and she was in Montana meant that it just wasn't doable for a fifteen-year-old. In retrospect, one thing I've learned is that when your close friend is in pain, you need to be there. No matter what.

But one thing is certain: I couldn't have protected her from what happened next.

Odd things were happening; Kristy would call me and explain that a young woman she had never met was over at their house all the time with her dad. The woman was in her thirties, with long, dark-brown hair, piercing eyes, and a wicked smile. Her name was Maya.

Maya was a dental assistant working in Bozeman. Kristy wasn't sure what Maya's connection was to her dad, but she didn't like it. Maya was making funeral plans for her mother! Kristy wondered, *Who is this woman, and why is she interfering in a very personal matter, and at a very difficult time like this?*

It may have been morbid to think about, but when I was in Montana I distinctly remembered Emily saying she wanted to be cremated when she died. Although I didn't attend the funeral, Kristy and other family friends told me it was quite the event. Two of Emily's horses were walked beside her casket on the way to the burial site. She was not cremated. Flowers were everywhere, and there were even violinists playing. Her tombstone was elaborate, with etched horses and kind words. It was all a little over-the-top for someone in her family.

After the funeral, Kristy decided to go searching for answers about her mother. She spoke with Emily's coworkers, who helped fill in the missing pieces: Emily had planned to confront James that evening after the kids' concert. She suspected that James was having an affair. If he admitted to it, Emily had plans to pack her bags and take the kids with her. By some twist of fate, because she died in the car accident she was never able to confront James.

It turned out Maya was James's mistress, and their affair was only the beginning. A month passed after the funeral, and Maya was still coming by the house. Kristy and Brent began comforting each other, because they felt like they didn't know their dad anymore. He was ignoring them—he was too busy with Maya.

Shortly after the funeral, in the middle of the school year, James sold the farmhouse and moved the kids to Bozeman. When Emily died, James became a rich man overnight. With her life insurance policy, he bought a new house in Bozeman.

One day, James came home early and told Kristy and Brent that there was something very serious he needed to talk about. He confessed that he had been having an affair with Maya before Emily died. He told them he had no intention of hurting them, but that he and Emily had fallen out of love. They had been distant for months. When James was at his six-month checkup at the dentist, he met Maya. She was young, beautiful, vibrant, and made James feel like he was on top of the world. They began seeing each other. Emily hadn't noticed since she was spending so much time helping her friend who was fighting cancer.

A month after Emily's funeral, Maya discovered she was pregnant. Maya didn't want the baby and demanded that James pay for an abortion. If he didn't, she threatened to tell his kids about the affair. James paid for the abortion. His guilt was weighing heavily on him, so he decided to tell Kristy and Brent the whole story. He ended his relationship with Maya after the abortion.

James was dealing with the death of his wife along with the guilt flowing through his mind because of the affair. It's hard to imagine what was going on in his head. He decided to go back to school to finish getting his bachelor's degree. With that decision, he transformed back into a college frat boy, staying out late at bars. At first Kristy was worried about him. She would go driving around town to find him in the morning. She often found him sleeping in his car outside the bar. On the positive side, he was smart enough not to drive home. This became a normal part of Kristy's life.

Not only were Kristy and Brent trying to deal with losing their mother; now they were trying to wrap their heads around the idea that their "hero," their father, had cheated on their mother and had been living a lie.

It was too much: the tragic death of her mother, the lies of her father, Maya getting pregnant and having an abortion…Kristy decided to get away from everything and planned to take a trip to Europe during the spring semester of her junior year of high school. This trip was actually something she had been talking about with her mother before she died. Under normal circumstances, a semester in Europe would have been an amazing opportunity for her. But now, with everything she was dealing with, what she really needed was some stability and normalcy.

CHAPTER 5
CHANGES

It was the summer after Emily's death, and I just had to see Kristy. She had been through so much in the past ten months that I was aching to see her. I knew things would be different, but I needed to spend some time with her.

Luckily, my uncle and aunt from Seattle drove to South Dakota for a few weeks' vacation with our extended family. They were heading back, and once again they let me ride with them in their BMW, since they were driving through Bozeman on their way back to Seattle. Kristy had moved to Bozeman with her dad and brother for the summer. We met at a gas station just off of the interstate. I saw her pull up in a cute yellow car. I could immediately tell that she had changed a lot from the last time I saw her.

We hugged, and I almost started crying. It was like I could feel her pain. All I wanted to do was make it better for her. She drove us to the new house that her dad had bought. It was in a nice neighborhood near the mountains on a beautiful and peaceful street with a few other houses. While I was staying there, I would get up in the morning, make breakfast, and sit outside on the deck, taking in the beautiful scenery of green grass, colorful flowers, and fresh mountain air.

One morning I was up before Kristy. James hadn't left for work yet.

"How long are you staying here?" he asked me.

"I'm not sure…I guess we didn't really plan how to get me back to South Dakota," I replied with a smile. James always intimidated me, so I would crack jokes to make myself feel more comfortable.

"Well, maybe you girls should drive to South Dakota and stay with your parents for a while; I won't be around for a few weeks, and I'd rather not have you girls here while I'm gone."

"That sounds good to me!" I said.

While we were in Bozeman, we drove to a coffee shop downtown every day. We bummed around, mostly, doing what most teenage girls do. One day we drove out to a famous actor's ranch because Kristy's brother Brent was working there all summer. This actor was not well liked in the community. Kristy explained that his wife had driven into town one day and told everyone that he had beaten her up during an argument. So the local townspeople didn't like this actor; there was no patience for a man who hit his wife—famous actor or not. The townspeople also didn't like celebrities coming in and buying land when they didn't live in the area. I guess they felt that local people who truly appreciated it should own the land. It was good to see Brent, too, but I could tell he had also grown up quickly with what he had been through.

So, after being in Bozeman for a few weeks, we decided to drive back to my parents' house in South Dakota. I loved that little yellow car. We packed up our stuff, got up really early, and made plans to drive all the way to Canistota, South Dakota, from Bozeman—a twelve-hour drive. We were still only sixteen, so we weren't able to get a hotel room on the way to Canistota. Kristy had to drive the entire way because her yellow car was a stick shift, and I didn't know how to drive a stick at that time. We had a blast driving those eight hundred miles, listening to music and talking about our future plans, boys, and school.

After we drove through Rapid City and the Black Hills, we encountered a semi driver who seemed to be following us. He would drive up real close to the back of our car and then slow down. He did this repeatedly. Then he would speed up and pass us, and while he was passing us he would honk his horn. Then he would slow down, and we would have to pass him.

When we passed him, we noticed he was talking on his radio system while honking at us. We were smart girls, so we knew we needed to write down his license plate number, and we did, just in case we needed it. We started to get really uncomfortable, but luckily we had to stop for gas.

We thought we had lost that crazy truck driver, but when we got back on the interstate, we encountered another semi driver who passed us and honked his horn. We noticed he was also talking on his radio system. We knew it was a different semi and a different guy, but the same behavior. We figured out that the truck drivers must have been talking about us on their radios! Well, for a while we felt like we were in the clear and had lost them. Then it started to rain. As luck would have it, the windshield wipers stopped working. It wasn't a sprinkle, either—it was a downpour. We couldn't see and had to pull off the road. We didn't have money or time to get the windshield wipers fixed, so we called my mom from Kristy's built-in cell phone in her car. We must have been in a somewhat populated area, because the call actually went through. My mom told us to get to a gas station and buy a can of water-repellent stuff that is made for windshields. We didn't even know something like that existed. Luckily, we found a big gas station and got a can of the water-repellant stuff. It worked like a charm! The water wiped right off the windshield, so we were able to keep driving.

After we lost the truck drivers and didn't have any more car issues, we made it safely to my parents' house. Kristy stayed with my family for a few weeks—and it wasn't all pleasant. For starters, Kristy and my seven-year-old younger brother didn't always get along. They would fight about what to watch on TV, or my brother would be stubborn about something. It was as if they were siblings. I have always been pretty protective of my brother and also of Kristy, so when they started fighting I didn't know what to do. Most of the time one of my parents would step in and break it up.

Like most teenage girls, we found interesting ways to entertain ourselves. We were both pretty boy crazy, so we went where the boys were. Most evenings, we would drive to Salem, which is a little larger than my hometown of Canistota. There were always teenagers driving around at night, going in a circle around the main street. I'm sure it had to drive the adults crazy having these teenagers driving down Main Street, honking at cute girls, and once in a while stopping and chatting. Kristy and I were quite the spectacle because we didn't go to school in Salem, so we were like fresh meat to the boys there. We met a couple of cute boys who were driving this old fifties convertible. We thought it would be fun to ride in a convertible, so we flirted with them. They offered to drive us around.

The following day, we drove to Salem and rode around with the guys in their convertible. We had a blast; it was a beautiful South Dakota summer day. I don't think we really did anything all day except drive around and talk. Kristy and I weren't really interested in dating these guys, but they were fun to hang out with.

We went back to my parents' house and had dinner. Then, at some point, my parents started to argue. I don't know what they were fighting about, but Kristy and I didn't want to stay at the house and listen to them argue. So we just left. That was the first time I had ever snuck out of the house. We drove to Salem to hang out with those boys again. We drove around for quite some time, and then we made a pit stop at a motel in Salem. I think we had stopped to talk to someone, and while we were talking, a Swedish couple who was traveling though South Dakota started to talk to us as well. They were traveling across the whole country. Since Kristy wanted to travel to Europe, she engaged this couple in a long conversation. The next thing we knew, it was 2:00 a.m. We were tired, so we headed back to my parents' house.

When we got there, the front door was locked. That was really weird, because my parents rarely locked the doors. So then we went around to the deck to try to get in through the side door. No such luck. Luckily, my mom didn't lock the door down by the basement. My older brother was sleeping downstairs, and we woke him up.

"You guys are in so much trouble!" Troy said.

"What do you mean?" I asked.

"You left and didn't tell Mom and Dad, and it's like two in the morning. Mom is pissed," he said.

Well, I figured it would be fine, so we went to sleep. The next morning, my mom came storming into my room.

"*Get out of bed!*" she yelled as she ripped the blankets off of me.

I looked at her with shock. I had never seen my mom so angry before.

"If you think you can just stay out until all hours of the night and not tell me where you are going," she continued to yell.

"You and dad were fighting, so we left. What's the big deal?" I countered.

By this time, my younger brother had come into the room. He looked concerned and didn't understand what was happening.

"I have a whole list of chores for you and Kristy to do today, and they better all be done by the time I get home!" she yelled. She handed me the list and slammed the door behind her. *Wow. She really means business*, I thought. Meanwhile, my older brother came upstairs and just started laughing at me. He had never seen me get into trouble, so this was pretty entertaining for him.

I looked at the list with Kristy:

–Clean all four bathrooms
–Vacuum

–Wash the floors
–Dust
–Clean the garage
–Clean out the refrigerator
–Clean the outside windows

Yowza! I thought. It would take us at least two days to finish all of this! It normally took us a full day just to clean out the garage. I was trying to figure out how to get this all done when Kristy suggested that we get my younger brother to clean the garage.

"Hey, Cody. How about helping us clean the garage?" Kristy asked.

"No way!" Cody replied.

"What if we made it worth your while? What would you want in return?" Kristy said.

"Peppermints!" Cody yelled. He loved those things. So we drove to Canistota and got him a large bag of peppermints. Luckily, he came through for us and cleaned out the entire garage. Who knew it would be that easy!

When my mom came home after work, she was really impressed that we had gotten everything done. We were exhausted. Lesson learned!

After our little "accident" in Montana with the Jeep, I was nervous about driving. Kristy was getting annoyed with me, so she decided that I needed to learn how to drive her yellow car. Driving a stick shift is much more complicated than driving an automatic transmission car; you have to know how to use the clutch and shift.

So one day Kristy drove me out onto our gravel road and had me give it a try. Let's just say she wasn't a very good teacher. I really didn't know what I was doing, and I stalled the car about five times.

"Oh my God! You aren't doing it right!" she yelled.

"I don't know what I'm doing!" I yelled back.

"You are going to damage my car!" she said. "Just stop. I'm going to drive."

Kristy didn't have much patience. Fair enough—I certainly didn't want to damage her car. Months later, my cousin successfully taught me how to drive a stick-shift car. The key is to slowly take your foot off of the clutch as you get started.

It was a great summer, and I was very thankful to be able to spend some time with Kristy, especially considering everything she had been through. She may have gotten me into a bit of trouble, but my parents still saw her as their child. My mom, in particular, took Kristy under her wing.

Kristy and my mom would stay up late talking—just the two of them. I know my mom was really worried about her, because I kept telling her about everything that had been happening in Kristy's life since her mom died. James's erratic behavior, the affair, the abortion, James moving into a new house...All of those things would be a lot to handle in a normal situation, but

Kristy and Brent were also trying to deal with the death of their mother. At one point, my mom called James to check in and let him know how Kristy was doing while she was staying with us.

"James, you know that you are all Kristy and Brent have now," she told him. "This has been a very difficult time for all of you, but it's been especially hard on your kids. Your kids need you. You have to be there for them."

James didn't say much in return and was probably annoyed that my mom had said something. But he really needed to hear it. It didn't change anything, unfortunately, but my mom couldn't sit back and say nothing. His behavior and actions had had devastating effects on his children.

I know now that everyone grieves differently—that everyone handles difficult situations differently—but at some point, you've got to pick yourself up, forgive yourself, and push forward. If you have kids, this is even more important because you have other human beings who are depending on you to be there for them. It doesn't mean that you always have to be strong, but you've got to refocus on what really matters. Almost always, what really matters is right in front of you. You can't live your life thinking of only yourself. Your actions and choices affect others. If we wallow in our own sorrows, we miss what life is offering us. Life is a journey (I'm sure everyone has heard that term), but it's the truth. There are ups and downs, straight, smooth paths, and very treacherous, curvy roads. We are presented with choices. Sometimes we make the right ones, and sometimes we don't. But the bottom line is, life is about teaching us things and teaching others. You will experience death, new beginnings, love in various forms, and a whole slew of other things! Your journey is your own, but we live in a world full of other people and creatures. Don't be blind to others who are around you.

It's amazing how quickly things can change in life.

CHAPTER 6
THE SUMMER BEFORE SENIOR YEAR OF HIGH SCHOOL

Before Kristy's mom died, they had made plans for Kristy to travel to Europe for about three months. Kristy was dealing with so much chaos in her life that she really did need to get away. She wanted to stick to her original plan. The only problem was that her emotional state wasn't the best. Combined with the standard teenage hormones, it was a recipe for a whole lot of mischief.

"Curious Kristy" turned into "Confident Kristy" in just a few months. While in Europe, she experimented with drugs, alcohol, and sex. She came back to the United States as a new young woman with a tattoo on her back, a bad smoking habit, and out-of-control, risk-taking behaviors. She was only seventeen but was taking the world by storm.

When she got back from Europe, she drove to South Dakota in her little yellow hatchback that we called Tweety (as in Tweety Bird). She planned to visit me and stay with my parents for a few weeks in the summer.

We were bored, and in true teenage girl fashion, we started talking about boys. Kristy was thinking about Austin, the boy on whom she had a crush for many years growing up. He was a bit of Casanova, and she wanted to get back at him because he would tease and taunt her but never actually date her.

So we decided to play a game with Austin. Kristy came up with a devious idea: we would get Austin really drunk—to the point where he would pass out—and then we would take off all of his clothes and leave him in a cornfield. The funniest part of our plan was that the closest house to this particular cornfield was his grand-parents' house! It seemed like a grand plan—or so we thought. Looking back now, however, it would have been horrible to leave a passed-out boy naked in a cornfield.

To start out our grand plan, Kristy began writing anonymous love letters to Austin. We wrote them for about three weeks—a letter every other day. In the last letter, Kristy wrote, "I think it's time for us to meet. I want you. Meet me at the center line on the football field at eight p.m. on Saturday night. Bring condoms."

So Saturday night rolled around. Kristy conned one of her dad's friends into buying beer for her. She loaded up her car with the beer and headed out to the football field to meet Austin. My job was to hang back at my parents' house until she called. Then I was supposed to go out to the football field to help her with Austin.

I waited patiently at my parents' house. Kristy had an old built-in cell phone in her car. At the time I didn't have a personal cell phone. We didn't think it would take too much time to get Austin drunk. Kristy thought it would only take two hours. I relied on her expertise when it came to drinking because I didn't drink at all. I was expecting her phone call around 10:00 p.m. And so I waited. Ten o'clock came and went. I started to get nervous. I thought maybe she had changed her mind about our plan. Or maybe she and Austin were having such a great time that they decided to become an item. Or maybe it was just taking longer to get Austin drunk.

Around eleven the phone rang.

"Kristy?" I asked impatiently.

"Yeah, it's me," she replied.

"So did you get Austin drunk? Are you ready for me to come out there with you?" I asked hastily.

"I slept with Lucas," she said.

"*What?* Lucas? You slept with Lucas?" I was so confused. Lucas was Austin's older brother. He was a Casanova too. He was tall, with blond hair and blue eyes, and he was always more sociable than Austin.

"Yes," she said.

"I don't understand. You were supposed to sleep with Austin, not Lucas. Sleeping with Lucas was not part of the plan. You need to stick to the plan. Do not deviate from the plan," I rambled.

Kristy laughed.

I let out a large sigh. "Okay, what the hell happened?"

"Well, Austin didn't show up. I guess he was too chicken to come out to the football field, so he told Lucas about the letters and asked Lucas to go instead," Kristy explained.

"Ah...okay. But why did you have sex with him?" I was so totally confused.

"Well, I was in this sexy outfit, and I was horny," she explained.

Being a sweet, innocent virgin, I couldn't comprehend this at all. But I'd learned not to question Kristy. She did what she wanted. I didn't always agree with her choices—and most of them I just didn't understand—but one thing was for sure: we were polar opposites.

Kristy came home late that night. Her little rendezvous with Lucas was short-lived; neither had the intention to make a relationship out of it, even though their families were close.

I'm not sure if Lucas ever told Austin what happened, but Kristy told Lucas not to tell Austin that they had slept together. It seems that Austin missed out on his chance.

As if our Austin plan wasn't enough, the summer continued to be filled with drama. Kristy heard about a wedding going on in a nearby town. In small towns, everyone comes out for the dance, even kids who don't have any idea who the bride and groom are.

We told my parents that we were going to this wedding dance and that we'd be home by midnight. My mom always told me to call her if I ever needed a ride home—no matter what time it was.

The dance was fun at first, and I met a few fun girls. Kristy was more preoccupied with flirting with some new guys. I watched her do her thing: tilt her head, smile and laugh, stick out her boobs, and hike up her shirt. She was flirting with a group of guys this time, and they seemed like trouble to me, so I avoided going over. I was having fun dancing with my new friends. The next thing I knew, I turned and noticed that Kristy was gone, and so were the guys. I had a sneaking suspicion that they were off doing drugs. So I continued to dance for a while, figuring Kristy would come back. Another hour came and went, and my new friends all decided to leave. I didn't know anyone else at the dance. I walked around looking for Kristy, but I couldn't find her. I had the car keys, so I decided to walk back to the car. Still no Kristy. I got in the car and called my mom. I asked her to come pick me up because Kristy had ditched me, and I had no idea where she was. I left the keys in the car, just in case she came back. My mom picked me up, furious that Kristy had left me by myself. "Friends don't ditch each other," my mom said.

A few hours passed, and I went to sleep. Then our phone rang. I picked it up.

"Hello?" I asked.

"Put your brother on the phone," Kristy said.

"Kristy? Are you okay?" I asked.

"Put your brother on the phone right now," she demanded. I put the phone down and went downstairs to wake up my older brother.

"Troy, I don't know what's wrong, but Kristy is demanding to talk to you on the phone," I said.

My brother got up and talked to her. I don't know what was said, but the next thing I knew, my mom was awake and my brother was putting his coat on and heading out the door.

"What's going on?" my mom asked.

"I gotta go get Kristy," my brother said. "She's in jail."

"What? What happened?" my mom asked. I stood there quiet as a mouse.

"She got caught drinking," my brother said. So my brother went to get Kristy out of jail and then came back home.

The next morning, I wanted to know all about what had happened, but Kristy seemed reluctant to tell me. It was as if my brother and Kristy had suddenly developed some sort of bond.

"I don't want to talk about it," she said when I asked her. "It was the worst night of my life, and I don't want to end up in jail ever again." It sounded horrible; if Kristy was so scarred by her brief time in jail, it must have been bad—nothing else seemed to scare that girl.

But the short time that Kristy spent in jail didn't stop her from getting into trouble. While she was in Europe, she had picked up the horrible habit of smoking. She smoked only one kind of cigarette: Marlboro Reds. I couldn't stand people who smoked. My mom was a sales rep for Philip Morris for many years, even though she didn't smoke. We had hundreds of cartons of cigarettes in our garage that my mom would store between her sales stops. While this provided me every opportunity to smoke, I never did. I guess I just listened to all of the messages that I had heard growing up: "Smoking kills," "Smoking causes cancer," "Smoking causes wrinkles and aging," and the list goes on and on. With all of those negative messages, I couldn't fathom taking up smoking.

But Kristy was seventeen and wasn't old enough to smoke or purchase cigarettes; still, she always managed to get them from someone, somehow. She even tried to con my older brother into buying her some, but luckily, he stood up to her and refused. I'm pretty certain that she even asked my mom to buy her cigarettes! Thankfully, no one in my family would do it.

One day, while Kristy was staying with us, we drove into Canistota to see if anything exciting was happening and stopped at Total Stop, the main convenience/grocery store in Canistota. We picked up a few snacks and drinks, and as we were checking out, Kristy very calmly asked to purchase a pack of Marlboro Reds. The lady at the register used to babysit Kristy years ago when her family lived near Canistota. She asked Kristy for her ID, and after looking at it, she told her she wasn't old enough to purchase cigarettes.

"Oh, come on! I'm only a few months away from being eighteen," Kristy said. I could tell that this made the clerk very uncomfortable.

"Kristy, you don't need the cigarettes, and you aren't old enough. Let's just go," I said firmly. But she wasn't listening to me.

Kristy turned back to the lady and proceeded to plead for the cigarettes. "Come on! I'll make it worthwhile for you. I'll give you an extra twenty dollars cash," she said. I knew this woman was a single mother with three children and that extra cash was tempting to her.

"Kristy, I just can't do it. I could lose my job," she said. At this point, I was so annoyed and embarrassed that I walked out to the car, leaving Kristy continuing to beg for the cigarettes.

A few moments later, Kristy came back to the car. "Oh my God, she wouldn't sell me the cigarettes! I can't believe it," she said, all flustered. I kept my mouth shut. I was glad the lady hadn't sold the cigarettes to Kristy. It was illegal. I was so mad at Kristy for putting that clerk's job at stake for those stupid cancer-causing cigarettes.

The clerk must have been upset and told the store manager about the incident, because the next day the Total Stop owner called my mom and relayed to her what had happened.

Later that night, my mom pulled me aside and asked me what was going on. She told me what the owner had said. Kristy was banned from going into Total Stop for the rest of the summer. My parents were mortified. My dad didn't know what to do with Kristy, because his experience with us had been that we were pretty well-behaved kids. I was just thankful that they didn't ban me from the store. I was also thankful that they knew that I wasn't trying to get cigarettes for myself; I didn't want the whole town thinking I was smoking. Kristy learned her lesson: she couldn't always persuade people to do what she wanted, and if she didn't follow the law, there were consequences.

CHAPTER 7
A ROAD TRIP AND ANOTHER ACCIDENT

It was late August 1999, and Kristy and I decided to drive to Minneapolis for the Lilith Fair music festival. We were pumped! Sheryl Crow, Sarah McLachlan, Indigo Girls, Shawn Colvin—we needed to go to this festival. We got our tickets and made plans to stay with Kristy's cousin, Jennifer, in Minneapolis.

Lilith Fair was on a Wednesday, so we planned to go to Minneapolis on Tuesday. Our senior year of high school started the next Monday, so the plan was to go back to Canistota on Friday so that Kristy could drive back to Montana and I could get back home and ready for school.

Jennifer lived with her boyfriend in South Minneapolis in a charming third-floor duplex with big windows and white walls. The apartment was quaint, bright, and vintage-looking. We arrived on Tuesday evening and got settled in. The next morning we got ready to spend the entire day at Lilith Fair.

When we got there, a huge crowd greeted us. We were in line when the gates opened and the massive crowd flowed through the gates with us. I remember thinking it was like a huge herd of cattle! Once we got in, we walked around and stopped at all the booths. It was a beautiful day.

We figured out which stage Sheryl Crow was going to perform and camped out in front of it all day. We took turns holding our spot.

The whole day was a blast, and the music was the cherry on top! We sang and danced; this music festival was all about women, and it was a very powerful and unifying feeling being there that day.

The next day we bummed around Minneapolis, and Jennifer took us out to a few places to shop and eat.

On Friday, we decided to go to brunch before going back to South Dakota. We followed Jennifer to the brunch place since we were planning on driving directly home from the café. We were sitting at a stoplight in a residential area. When the light turned green, Jennifer drove through the intersection. We followed, and out of nowhere a green Honda flew right in front of us! We hit the green car's back end, smashing up the entire front end of Kristy's yellow car. Luckily, we were wearing our seat belts.

We managed to pull the car over to the side of the road. Jennifer saw what had happened and came over. The driver of the green car was our age. He said he was looking for a specific street and didn't see the red light. I thought the guy was a complete idiot. I mean, Jennifer drove through the intersection, and yet he didn't see us right behind her?

Oddly, there was a bad car accident just up the street at about the same time. One car was up on the sidewalk with its side up against a tree! There was a police car there along with an ambulance. Jennifer called the police after our accident, so we were waiting for them to arrive. Soon a police car drove up. The cop rolled down his window and said he'd come back for us. These cops were going to the other accident first. We waited for an hour before the police came back to write up an accident report. Kristy was smoking a cigarette. I told her to put it out and to hide her cigarettes, since that would have been another fine because she was only seventeen. Luckily the cops didn't see her smoking since she hid her cigarette pack before they got to our car.

In Minnesota, there is a "no fault" law, which means that both parties are equally responsible for damages. In other words, even though it was clearly the other person's fault—running a red light and hitting a car—in Minnesota it didn't matter. A police officer asked us if we needed medical attention. We felt fine at that time, so we said no. It was a good thing that neither of us was hurt—or so we thought.

We were exhausted. And now we didn't know how we were going to get back to South Dakota and how we were going to get Kristy back to Montana. We hopped in the back of Jennifer's car with our stuff and drove back to her apartment. Kristy's fun hatchback yellow car ended up being a total loss. It was hauled off to the car impound lot. It was sad to see that car destroyed; it was such a great little car.

When we got back to Jennifer's apartment, Kristy called her dad with the news of the accident. He was mad because he saw her as a problem child. After a few minutes of talking, James finally understood that the accident wasn't Kristy's fault. I called my mom after Kristy was done talking to her dad. She insisted that we go to the hospital to make sure we were physically okay. Because we felt fine, I thought she was overreacting.

The next day we decided to go visit the University of Minnesota campus to check out a few cool places that Kristy's cousin had told us about. Jennifer had to work, so Kristy and I were on our own. We figured out the bus system since there was a bus stop not far from Jennifer's apartment. We did a lot of walking that day, but in the afternoon I started to have severe neck pain.

"Kristy, my neck hurts really bad. Do you think we should go to the doctor?" I asked.

"Let's go check out one more place on campus and then see how you feel," Kristy replied.

An hour later, my neck pain had become unbearable. That's when we decided to make a stop at the Fairview Medical Center on campus. We walked in and explained our situation. We both had insurance through our parents, so I didn't expect any complications.

The medical staff was suspicious of us and didn't seem to believe our story. Apparently they didn't understand how we hit the other car, and they thought we were at fault and making up some crazy story. It was weird and very frustrating. They didn't treat me right away; in fact, we had to wait for hours. Once they called us, we met with a nurse. I could tell that she didn't believe our story. She suggested that we seek medical attention from our regular doctor. Lesson learned: when you are in a car accident, don't wait a few days to seek medical attention if you are on your own and under the age of eighteen.

I was so frustrated and angry at that point that we asked the nurse to speak with our parents. Kristy was able to get a hold of her dad, so James spoke with the nurse and confirmed our story. Then I had my mom talk to her as well. I told my mom that I was in pain and that the medical staff was questioning our story. My mom was annoyed.

"My daughter and her friend need to see a doctor. They were in a car accident yesterday. What is the problem?"

"We just wanted to verify their story; sometimes we have to call the police when a story doesn't add up with a minor," the nurse said. "We'll take good care of the girls."

I was flabbergasted that the medical staff didn't just help us right away and that we had to "clear our story" just to get medical attention. We met with a doctor who prescribed me pain pills. He said that I had whiplash. He said it wasn't a severe case, but boy, was I in pain. I have no idea how painful a severe case of whiplash would have been!

We stopped by the pharmacy and picked up the pills. I was grateful to have something to help with the pain. We got on the next bus back to Jennifer's apartment. I was in a total fog, so I went to bed shortly after we got back.

We decided to take a Greyhound bus back to South Dakota on Monday. They weren't running on the weekends, so this meant that I was going to miss the first day of school. The bus ride was long, and the bus was crowded with weird people. It made me thankful that our families could afford vehicles. It took six hours to get to Sioux Falls, when it would normally have taken us four hours by car. My mom and brother met us at the bus stop in Sioux Falls. I was so happy to see them!

James decided to pay for a plane ticket for Kristy to get back home, so the next day my mom drove her to the airport. Kristy made it back to Montana safely, and

I explained to everyone at school why I missed the first day. I had to be careful taking the pain pills; sometimes they made me feel nauseous and foggy.

My senior year of high school was a good one. There's a sense of authority that you gain as a senior in high school. You are getting ready to step into the real world and be an adult. Teachers and administrators at school treat you differently, with more respect, once you are a senior. At least that's how I felt.

I think it's safe to say that I wasn't considered one of the popular girls in high school. I wasn't the cool girl who everyone wanted to hang out with. I was friends with and was kind to everyone. What set me apart from my classmates was the fact that I didn't drink alcohol. Living in a small, rural town, drinking alcohol in high school was considered the norm. It didn't interest me. With my uncle dying from throat cancer and suffering from alcoholism, it made me not want to touch the stuff.

CHAPTER 8

YOUNG LOVE

Kristy flew back to Montana and got ready for her senior year of high school. I was excited for my last year of high school too!

During my junior and senior years, I worked at the Barnes & Noble Café, and I loved it. The backroom of the café was connected to the large shipping room, and a guy named Michael working there caught my eye. He seemed really nice, and he was cute, with blue eyes and short, blond, curly hair. We would briefly chat once in a while in passing, and then one day he asked me out on a date! I was so excited because I had never been on an official date before. We agreed to meet at the front of Barnes & Noble by the checkout counters the next weekend. I got there a little early and went to pick up my check. On my way back to the checkout counters, I found Michael there, looking a bit frantic.

"Oh good, you're here! I thought maybe you were going to ditch me. I've had other girls do that to me," he said with such honesty. I'm sure I had a confused look on my face as I assured him that I was happy to go on a date with him. Then he asked me if I wanted to drive or if he should drive.

"You can drive," I said immediately. I was still a little uncomfortable driving, and since I was the girl, I thought it was the guy's job to drive on a date. We walked out to the parking lot, and he pointed to his car: a black BMW! I think my mouth dropped. I was shocked and totally impressed.

Michael was a good guy, and I'm lucky that he was my first real boyfriend. I spent most of my senior year of high school in Sioux Falls, where Michael lived with his parents. I worked most weekends at Barnes & Noble, so after work I would hang out with Michael and his friends. Soon, Michael and I were officially boyfriend and girlfriend. News that I was dating spread quickly in my small-town school, not only a guy who was from Sioux Falls, but a guy who drove a BMW. The girls at school were suddenly interested in my social life. Every Monday, the popular girls would ask me what I did over the weekend. It was as if I became popular overnight. I was just happy that I had more interesting things to do than drink all weekend. I attended Michael's winter formal, and we attended both of our high school proms.

In the beginning of my senior year, I was still taking pain pills for my neck pain from the whiplash. I told Michael about it, and he talked to his dad, who was a dermatologist in Sioux Falls. He recommended that I see a certain orthopedic surgeon. I met with the orthopedic surgeon, and he had me do exercises to help strengthen the muscles in my neck. For example, he had me do specific neck movements with light weights. The good thing was that my neck started to feel better. To this day, if I'm under a lot of stress, my neck will start to hurt.

My senior year was a great one, but Kristy's was a different situation.

Brent had started at a new school in Bozeman, but Kristy didn't want to start a new high school during her senior year. James was focused on his own needs and didn't care what Kristy did, so he allowed her to live by herself in Ennis as she finished her last year of high school. Kristy still tried to reach out to her father, but James didn't want anything to do with her. He was focused on his own academics and being with his new wife. He was failing in his classes. When Kristy would come over on the weekends, James repeatedly told her that she was his problem. He took her to see a therapist and told the therapist to "fix her." I can't imagine how hurtful that must have been for her, to have her father call her a problem.

While in Europe, her dad had met a new woman, and their relationship grew quickly. Kristy had asked him to not marry her and to wait until she came back before taking such a drastic step so quickly. James, of course, didn't listen. He got married to a very controlling woman who didn't care about Kristy and Brent. She was a gold digger at heart. James bought her new cars, new jewelry, new clothes...It never seemed to be enough. James was spending all his time trying to please his new wife, who continued to find excuses why Kristy shouldn't spend so much time with them on the weekends. So Kristy saw her dad less and less frequently.

Kristy's grandparents, who lived in Bozeman, were no help. They were in denial that their precious son had done anything wrong; they sided with James and agreed that Kristy was a "problem child." James distanced himself from his only daughter, driving a canyon-sized gap between the two of them. Kristy needed her father; she needed support and love. So she went searching for a replacement.

Living on your own in your senior year of high school and having your world turned upside down equals trouble. Trouble's name was Connor. Kristy met him at the laundromat. He was older, with dark hair, a killer smile, crystal-blue eyes, and a body to die for. He worked for his family's construction company. Kristy fell hard for him. James was paying for Kristy's apartment, but she was staying with Connor most nights. Kristy would always say the best sex is with someone you love. Young hormones, strong physical attraction, and passionate personalities kept them together.

During Christmas break, I was in my parents' kitchen, baking Christmas cookies, when Kristy called with something really urgent to tell me. During one of Kristy and Connor's passionate sex episodes, the condom broke. And what luck, Kristy got pregnant.

It wasn't that Kristy didn't want children, nor was it that she didn't like children. Through all the emotional turmoil she had been through, she couldn't fathom the idea of having or raising a child. She didn't want a baby. Emotionally and mentally, she wasn't able to have a baby grow in her body. This was apparent when she told me that the very day she found out she was pregnant, she went out drinking. She and Connor knew that she had to have an abortion. She went through with it, and Connor was by her side. Even though it was difficult, for her, it was the best decision.

I've never been against abortion; I have always believed that there should be a choice. My grandfather's biological mother died trying to give herself an abortion. Her husband (my grandfather's biological father) was very abusive and didn't want any more children. So when she became pregnant with her third child, she used a wire coat hanger to try to perform an abortion. Sadly, she ended up bleeding to death. I learned at a young age that abortion is not a black-and-white decision. People usually just think about the unborn child, but they forget about the mother. Unless you are in that woman's shoes, you cannot and should not judge her decision. You have no idea what is going on in her life—her mental or emotional state. Some women are not able to carry a child in their body for nine months.

I often wonder why our society pushes women to get married and have children, as if you aren't truly doing your societal duty unless you have done both. I believe we should push our children—and specifically women—to wait to get married. The bottom line is each woman has her own path. Respect it. Embrace it. Encourage it.

CHAPTER 9

YOUNG ADULTHOOD

Kristy and I both graduated high school, and that was when real adulthood started. Kristy attended college at Bozeman State University and moved into the dorms. She had plans to become a veterinarian, so she was majoring in biology. She and Connor continued to see each other, but not as often as they would have liked. Connor was busy working various construction jobs and struggling with his own issues. He was known for getting into bar fights as well as drinking and driving. Soon it caught up with him. Kristy called me with the news.

"Connor got arrested last night. He beat up some guy at one of the local bars," she said with a sigh. "I don't know why he gets into these fights. Sometimes I think he might have a drinking problem."

"I'm pretty sure he has a drinking problem," I told her. "Don't you worry that this could be a sign that he could be abusive toward you?" I asked, concerned.

"No. He would never hit me. And if he did, he knows he'd be hit back twice as hard," she said with a chuckle. "I'm worried that he's acting out because I've been gone at school. We used to see each other every day…Now, I'm lucky if I see him once a week."

"Yeah, but Kristy, your education should be your top priority. This is about your future. Connor is an adult and has to take responsibility for his actions. Besides, he should be supportive that you want to get a college education," I replied.

Connor ended up in jail and eventually on probation. Kristy stuck with him for the time being, but she grew weary of their relationship.

I left my small hometown for the big city of Minneapolis, attending the University of Minnesota. Kristy and I kept in touch all the time. While Kristy and Connor's relationship started to fizzle, my relationship with my high school boyfriend began to waver as well.

Michael was going to school in Duluth, Minnesota, about two hours away from Minneapolis. We tried the whole "friends with benefits" thing. Then one weekend I needed to get to Duluth to see him, but I didn't have a car. So I caught a ride with two guys heading to Duluth. One of them, Jacob, caught my attention. He was smart, kind, and funny—and we had instant chemistry. Jacob knew I was in Duluth to see my boyfriend, but when we returned to Minneapolis, he asked me out on a date. I was honest with my boyfriend and told him that I had started dating Jacob. Big surprise—Michael no longer wanted to be "friends with benefits," and he wanted to start seeing me exclusively. I stayed in contact with Jacob and we remained friends.

Kristy and her dad began to heal their fractured relationship. James started to realize that his new wife shouldn't be keeping him from his kids, and even though this new wife didn't like Kristy, she was the only daughter he had.

Connor and Kristy each started to go their own way, with Kristy attending college and Connor working odd jobs for his family's construction company. It was becoming apparent that they were on different wavelengths and moving in different directions. By the end of the school year, Kristy decided that she needed to start over and wanted to move. She was also getting more serious about her education and was looking for a university that had an excellent veterinary program.

Kristy called me one evening. "Stacy, I'm seriously thinking about going to school at the University of Minnesota. I've already called a few people, and they said I could easily transfer my credits."

We decided to look for an apartment together.

Kristy left Montana and drove to South Dakota in her beat-up minivan. James's new wife wouldn't allow him to give Kristy a newer, safer vehicle. Kristy had plenty of money tied up in investments from her mother's insurance settlement, yet she couldn't access the funds; James had secured them by putting an age limit on when Kristy would be able to access them, so she was pawning various items for money in addition to working as a waitress.

Kristy packed up the van with items that she would need for the summer: flip-flops, shorts, tank tops, toiletries, swimsuits, CDs, and books. She left her other stuff with Connor, thinking she'd drive back to Montana at some point for the rest of her belongings. Even though their relationship was still rocky, she trusted him enough to leave some of her items with him.

In perfect Kristy fashion, she didn't tell me when she'd make it to South Dakota. My family and I were attending my cousin's wedding in Winner, and I had invited Kristy to attend, but I wasn't able to tell her where the wedding and reception were being held.

During the wedding reception, sure enough, Kristy showed up! She drove into Winner, stopped at a café, and asked people where the wedding was. She was always very resourceful. When she arrived at the reception, she didn't have any money left to pay for gas to drive the rest of the way to our house. My parents helped her out with some cash, and I drove back with her to our house.

CHAPTER 10

THE SUMMER MONTHS BEFORE THE ACCIDENT

Kristy was a wild child, a free spirit, independent, and strong-willed. She was dead set on attending the University of Minnesota with me in the fall of 2001 to pursue a degree in veterinary medicine with a minor in the Dutch language. She was starting to get back on track and was determined to make a better life for herself.

I had just finished my freshman year and was ready to move off campus. It seemed like a great idea for us to get an apartment together, although part of me was a little nervous of how that would go because we were so different, and at times we each needed our own space. During my freshman year, I was in a single dorm room with no roommates. I met some great people that year, but when Kristy said she really wanted to go to the university, it just made sense for us to get a place together.

On a whim, we drove to Minneapolis with very little money and no hotel reservations. Kristy was sure we could stay with her cousin, even though she was never able to get ahold of her. While we were waiting to hear back, we looked at five different apartments in different areas of Minneapolis.

By about 5:00 p.m., I told her that we needed a new plan and that we needed to figure out where we were going to stay the night. I called the only girl I knew who was still living on campus, Chloe, whom I'd met while living in the dorm. Our friendship started like a lot of college people's; I was looking for a table to eat breakfast at one morning and saw a girl sitting by herself. I asked if I could join her. She said yes, and from that moment on, we were friends. Chloe was a happy-go-lucky, high-energy, positive, and friendly person.

So there we were. I felt bad calling Chloe and asking her if we could stay with her for the weekend, but she, being the gracious young woman that she was, said yes.

Since we were in Minneapolis, I thought it would be fun to hang out with Jacob. I called him, and we ended up having a double date. Jacob and his friend Sam, along with Kristy and I, went out for a fun evening. We went out for dinner and saw a movie and then headed to a place to play pool. Kristy and I beat the boys at several games of pool. I actually sucked at playing pool, but Kristy kicked ass. Throughout the evening, Kristy was flirting with Jacob. It made no sense to me because Kristy never seemed to go for the guys I liked. We always had different tastes in men. Jacob still wanted to date me, so I think he saw Kristy's flirtations as an opportunity to make me jealous. It worked. By the end of the weekend, I was mad at Kristy for flirting with Jacob because I wanted him to myself.

On our last night in Minneapolis, one of Chloe's guy friends, Chris, who lived down the hall in her apartment building, came over and introduced himself. He and Kristy seemed to hit it off—not so much in a romantic sense, but as a friendship. I went to bed early on the floor, and later, Kristy slept next to me after she had been up for some time hanging out with Chris. I don't know what they were doing, or if they were drinking.

The next morning we had breakfast at a coffee shop. It was a beautiful morning, and I was reminded of how much I enjoyed the U of M campus and culture.

After breakfast, we packed up our stuff and started on our way back to South Dakota. It was hot, and I knew we didn't have air conditioning in the beat-up van, so I decided to put on my yellow bikini top with jean shorts. I chuckled as we drove through Minneapolis, feeling like I was in a drug dealer's van. People would turn to look, and then they'd see two cute girls. It was fun to watch their reactions.

Some of Kristy's mom's relatives lived in Minnesota, and since we were somewhat close, Kristy wanted to make an effort to see them. Specifically, she wanted to see her mom's parents. She pulled out a map, and we rerouted the drive out to her grandparents' farm. We got lost a few times, but eventually we made it. The only problem was that when we got to the farm, no one was there. Kristy peeked in the windows and checked out the farm buildings. I stayed in the van. She walked back with a confused look on her face.

"I don't get it," she said. "It's like they are gone, like, moved away gone." It was almost creepy that they weren't there. "I wonder what the heck happened. I guess they must have moved." It was sad that Kristy and her grand-parents hadn't stayed in touch.

I could tell she was disappointed. She rarely got to see her grandparents, especially after her mom's death. Word of James's cheating quickly circulated through the family. Plus, with Kristy and Brent living in Montana, and the other side of the family in South Dakota and Minnesota, they didn't see much of each other.

After trying to find Kristy's grandparents, and having no luck, we continued on our way to South Dakota. We drove most of the way in silence because I was still pissed at her for flirting with Jacob.

Kristy wanted to stop in Madison, where she and my brother lived, because she wanted to pick up some more clothes and stay the night at my house in Canistota. It was the day before July 4, and my family always had a get together for my older brother's birthday.

We were starving, so we stopped at a Subway to pick up food, and then we headed to my brother's house. We saw my brother for a couple of minutes, and Kristy took her sweet time gathering up a few items. Then she got on the computer and started checking her e-mail and playing the song "I Want to Fuck You Like an Animal." I remember her singing along as she blasted the music throughout the house. That song always made me cringe. Fuck you like an animal? Uh, no thanks.

We got back in the van and headed to the gas station before leaving Madison. We started to sing along with a Sheryl Crow song on the radio and act really crazy, like we always used to when we were younger. She always knew how to make me laugh, and then I wasn't pissed at her anymore. I really appreciated our friendship in that moment.

As we drove, we had the windows down because the van didn't have air conditioning. I was still wearing my yellow bikini top and shorts, and Kristy was wearing a white shirt and black capris. When we got to Highway 81, we had to make a sudden turn, and Kristy forgot that it came up fast. She slammed on the brakes, and I felt as if the van was about to flip. I was laughing inside and said jokingly, "Nice turn there."

Kristy never did have good luck with cars. I was staring out the window at the green fields when a song by

No Doubt and Lil' Kim came on the radio. I turned to watch Kristy sing while she held her cigarette. I had taken off my sandals because I wanted to sit with my legs crossed on the seat. I had a brief thought of what would happen if we got into an accident. Looking back, that's a very creepy thought, because shortly after that thought crossed my mind, we were indeed in the accident that ended Kristy's life and changed mine forever.

CHAPTER 11

AFTER THE ACCIDENT

My parents didn't have money. I paid my way through college and learned how to financially support myself at a young age. I always had a job and never borrowed money from my parents.

A few days after the accident, after I got back from the hospital, a lawyer named Mike showed up at my parents' house. I was still distraught and in shock. He said he was Kristy's dad's attorney. Since James lived in Montana, he sent his lawyer out to South Dakota to talk to me. He started asking me all these questions. "Were you girls drinking?" he asked sternly.

"No," I replied calmly.

"You sure?" he asked.

"Yes. We left in the morning. We walked down the street on the main street of campus to eat breakfast before we left. We ate a few pastries and had coffee," I said, thinking back to that day.

"Were you wearing your seat belt?"

"Yes. It left a mark on me," I replied and showed him my scars.

"Was Kristy wearing her seat belt?"

I had to think about that. "I think so…I thought she was wearing it, but I don't know. I guess she wasn't wearing her seat belt since she was obviously thrown from the vehicle," I replied, trying to be helpful. "I guess I don't know what happened to her. I don't know how everything happened. It just happened so fast."

"What do you remember?" Mike asked.

"We were driving down Highway 81, and all of sudden I turned and I saw this green tractor loader coming right at us. Then I turned to look at Kristy to make sure she saw what was happening. She turned the wheel and screamed," I said.

Mike turned to my parents to explain the rest of the story. "The kid that was driving the tractor was ten years old. His parents allowed him to drive the tractor. He was crossing the highway to pick up a bale of hay, and for whatever reason, he didn't see you. I went out to the crash site and found the tire marks from the van. The tractor loader head cut through the van like can opener. It hit Kristy in the chest with such force that it broke her seat and the seat belt. At the same time the back doors opened, and Kristy flew out. She died instantly when the loader hit her chest. She didn't suffer."

I started to cry. My parents told Mike that was probably enough for the day. He asked if he could ask me more questions later, and I told him that would be fine.

The day I came home from the hospital is a day I will never forget. It was July 4—my older brother's birthday. I told him that I didn't get him a birthday present. That my present was me—alive!

I remember feeling so lucky. I sat down to eat a bowl of cereal, and I was in such an utter state of happiness. *I'm alive! I'm alive, and I can eat cereal! I can feed myself! I can walk! I still have my legs, my arms, my fingers, my toes!* It was euphoria, followed by bleak sadness. My very best friend was dead. It was too much for my mind to comprehend, so I shut out the sadness and focused on getting myself back to normal.

Looking in the mirror was something that I avoided after the accident. I didn't look like myself at all. I had two swollen black eyes, like something that you would see if you had been punched in the face two times. My entire face was puffy, red, and swollen and covered with cuts. Basically, I looked like someone had beaten the shit out of me. I thought to myself, *Geez, I wonder if I will ever look like myself again. If not, I wonder if I can afford plastic surgery.*

When it was time for the funeral, my whole family packed into my mom's small car. There were five of us: my mom, dad, my older brother, me, and my younger brother. We drove to Bozeman for the funeral. During our drive, when we stopped at gas stations, I remember the smell of gasoline made me sick to my stomach. It reminded me of being in the van right after the accident and smelling the gas, scared that the van might blow up like in the movies.

When I walked into the gas stations to use the bathroom, I noticed that people just stared at me. People's eyes would bug out, and they would have this concerned look. Then they would turn away and avoid looking at me. At one gas station, I walked in with my older brother, who was tall, over six feet, and rock solid. The lady at the counter looked at me, and then looked at my brother. I figured she thought he beat me up, so I made sure to smile so she knew I wasn't being abused. I started to get used to the strange looks and got a serious reality check that life isn't about how you look; it is what is inside that matters. I would remember to hold my head up and smile and not be ashamed of how I looked. Life is really about people, anyway, not what we look like. Besides, who the fuck cares what I look like when I've just been in an accident and my best friend died?

On our drive to Montana, my mom was busy making phone calls. She remembered that a female lawyer who specialized in car accidents had a cabin next to my aunt's cabin at Swan Lake. My aunt gave my mom the lawyer's information, and away my mom went. She was able to get an appointment for the following week.

When we got to Bozeman, I started to reminisce. "Oh, this coffee place is where Kristy and I would go every day!" I explained. "And that place right there, that's where we went shopping." My family was quiet. They were probably wondering why I wasn't crying. I was still in total shock and so utterly thankful that I was alive.

Once we arrived at the funeral, reality started to set in. I hugged Kristy's dad. And I cried. I hugged Kristy's grandma and sobbed. It was as if a constant stream of water was coming out of my eyes.

There was a guest book and a big display with pictures of Kristy. Everyone was signing and writing messages on the display. I wrote, *Best friends forever. Love your soul sister Stacy.*

I sat with my family a few pews behind James and Brent. At the front was a pink urn. I turned to my brother and said, "The urn is pink. It should be blue. Kristy's favorite color was blue." My brother half chuckled and said that there wasn't much we could do right now to change that.

My mom said she was sorry that Kristy had been cremated, thinking it would be better for me to see the body. My mom had written down several things that she wanted to say during the funeral. I also had a few things I wanted to say. When the time came, I was unable to speak. I couldn't stop crying. I sobbed through the entire funeral, so much so that I don't remember a word that anyone said. I remember my mom pulled out a piece of paper and read a few things on my behalf. I kept thinking, *This is not happening. How can I be sitting here at my best friend's funeral? I never thought I'd be nineteen years old sitting at my best friend's funeral. This is some kind of horrible, tragic mistake.*

But it wasn't a mistake. It was very real.

When we went to the burial, I told myself I needed to get it together. That I couldn't continue to sob constantly. Before they covered up the urn with dirt, I threw in a necklace. One half had the word "Best," and the other half had "Friend."

I was exhausted. I had cried so much, I was starting to get dehydrated, and all I wanted to do was sleep. I told my parents that I didn't want to go back to the church to eat. "How can people eat at a time like this?" I asked, disgusted. "I'm not hungry at all." My mom said that people would like to talk to me and that we should remember that the funeral was for everyone, not just me.

So we went back to the church and I had some juice. People started to come up to me. Kristy's grandparents from her mother's side gave me their condolences. They said they had a lot going on and felt bad that they hadn't kept in touch with Kristy. They said they had recently moved off the farm in Minnesota and into town. *Well, that explains it,* I thought. Kristy had driven out of her way to her grandparents' farm on the way back to South Dakota from Minneapolis, just to see them. I didn't have the heart to tell them that had happened. It would have made them feel guiltier than they already felt.

Suddenly, I realized that Kristy's boyfriend Connor was not there. I ran over to Brent, Kristy's brother, and said, "Oh my gosh, did anyone tell Connor about Kristy? She would have wanted him to be here. He should be here." I was very upset. He said that he had notified Connor, but that James would not have wanted him to be there, so he'd told Connor not to come.

When we got back to the hotel, I fell asleep on the bed. My family wanted to do a bit of sight-seeing, since we had driven so far, and the rest of my family had never been to Montana. So we ended up driving to a few tourist places around Bozeman the next day. Then we headed home to South Dakota.

A few days later, I met with my new lawyer, Sabrina. My parents came with me, and as we started talking, we mentioned that James's attorney had already visited me at my parents' house. Sabrina looked shocked and said that he should never have done that. We gave her his name and contact information. She said she would be in touch with him and that we should not speak to him without her present. Then she had her assistant take photos of my face and scars.

She suggested that I go in and have x-rays taken from all angles. This was to ensure that the doctors didn't miss anything. She said sometimes medical professionals are only focused on the main areas, and in her experience, she had seen issues missed in other clients. X-rays from all angles would ensure that we had everything covered.

I left her office thankful that she had my best interests at heart. My parents really didn't have a clue as to what to do next.

I went to the doctor's office and had the x-rays. My lawyer also suggested that I keep a journal noting all of my medical issues over the next year. She explained to me that sometimes injuries take a while to appear.

I was good about writing in my journal. I included things about the accident, things that I'd remember, dreams, my mental state; it got me thinking that perhaps someday I would write a book.

I learned quickly that most legal situations don't get resolved very fast—they are slow-moving, like molasses.

When things started to settle in my mind, I realized that James really had no idea what his daughter was like or what she was doing or trying to achieve. So I took the reins and started contacting people about Kristy's death. I called to cancel her upcoming doctor's appointment; I contacted Yahoo to close her e-mail account; I contacted the University of Minnesota to let them know that Kristy had died; I went through her belongings that were in South Dakota and gave some to her friends. Then it struck me that she had told me she had a will. I looked through everything I could, just in case she had brought it with her to South Dakota. I had no idea if she actually went to an attorney to put the will together, but I distinctly remembered the day she told me about it.

It was the summer after her mother had died. Obviously, death was on her mind; most sixteen-year-olds don't think about creating a will. But with her mom's passing and now having a trust and investments and her dad behaving like a teenager, she wanted to make sure that the things that were most important to her were given to those closest to her.

"I want you to know that I have a will," she said as she was driving me in her yellow car.

"Okay," I said.

"Yep…you, my brother, and Connor are all in it," she explained.

"Well, that's good to know," I replied, not wanting to pry into what she was leaving me.

"Connor helped me put it together the other night, and you are included," she said very seriously, but with a smile.

I nodded in understanding, but didn't ask anything more about it. Now I wished I would have asked more questions, such as *Where is it located—in a safe? A security box at a bank? Tucked away with your personal items? Hidden in a journal? Is it with Connor?* Things that at the time I didn't think were important, but now I regret not asking more questions. To this day, we have never found her will.

CHAPTER 12
BACK TO COLLEGE

About three weeks after the accident, I started having back problems. It hurt around my right shoulder and down my lower back. I thought about going to see a chiropractor, but within a couple of days the pain went away. After the back pain ceased, I had something like muscle spasms in my left ankle and my right calf. They didn't last long, but they tingled, and I couldn't walk until it stopped. The spasms lasted only a couple of days or so. Then, like the back pain, they stopped.

I continued to track any pain or symptoms at the direction of my lawyer. She wanted to make sure I carefully logged it, since often physical issues can occur months, or even years, after an accident.

Kristy and I had gone to Minneapolis to find an apartment for the fall semester. Now it was the middle of July, and I had no place to live. So I did what I do best: I reached out to all my contacts. In my e-mail to everyone I knew in Minneapolis, I explained what had happened (this was before Facebook and Myspace) and my current situation. Luckily, I got a break! One of my friends worked with a girl who was looking for a roommate in a house to share with a few other girls. I contacted her and set up a date to take a look.

In early August 2001, my mom and I drove to Minneapolis and checked out the townhouse, which was like huge apartments all in one large building. The outside looked pretty crappy, and the hallway connecting all of the townhouses was gross. Then we got to the door, which had "Introducing Lucky Number 8" on it in sparkly stickers.

The inside was surprisingly nice: wood floors, a big kitchen, a huge living/dining room, an upstairs with three bedrooms and two bathrooms, and a downstairs with a washer and dryer and plenty of space for a bedroom.

The girl I met was named Anna, and both of her parents were there as well. As it turned out, Anna was actually the one who was looking for a roommate since she was the person who had secured the townhouse. She was nice, and I thought we could be good friends. Anna and the other two girls gave me a tour. We went downstairs, where in the corner I noticed a huge stuffed animal: a giant pink pig. I asked what the pig was about.

One of them said she'd won it at the fair. My mom and I looked at each other. We knew Kristy was giving me a sign. After looking around and deciding that I could live in the basement, I signed the contract. I was relieved to have a place to live in the fall.

Three weeks later, my parents and brothers helped me move. I was ready to get on with my life and continue my education. It was hard when my parents left that day, though, because I had leaned on them so much over the last two months. They were my strongest supporters.

My roommates, I'm sure, had no idea the impact they would have on me. Even though I'd met a lot of people my freshman year, I hadn't really become close friends with any of them. And why would I, when I had a best friend? Now that my best friend was gone, I had to readjust, picking new friends and figuring out whom I could trust and depend on.

Olivia was tall, lanky, smart, and boyish, yet she wore makeup. Zoe was spunky, short, happy-go-lucky, and very intelligent. Anna was easygoing, kind, smart, and funny. We were like a family. Olivia and Zoe had been in a sorority together, so they were good friends prior to moving into the townhouse with Anna and me. Anna and I became friends instantly, and to this day, we remain very close.

Anna and I were goofy; we laughed a lot and had fun. We baked cookies on a weekly basis. The problem was we would eat most of the cookie dough, so we never ended up making that many cookies. We even got mono together—we're pretty sure that while we were both eating cookie dough out of the same bowl, one of us infected the other!

Journal, Fall 2001

The more I think about the accident, the more I realize how lucky I was. I miss Kristy. I am in my new townhouse. I am happy here, but at the same time it would have been good to have been rooming with my best friend. I put up some pictures of her in my room. My mom keeps saying that it still feels like a dream, that she can't believe Kristy's gone. It doesn't feel like that for me. I know she's gone. I keep thinking that I need to contact Connor, Kristy's boyfriend. Connor wasn't at the funeral, and it bothered me, because I know that Kristy would have wanted him to be there. It makes me nervous when I think about James, because I don't know what he is going to do regarding suing the kid's family. I hope that he doesn't. I have had a couple of friends ask me why I wasn't going to sue them, but I just feel that won't solve anything. All it will do is cause more pain to the kid's family. But I do want everything to be covered. If I do get a large settlement, it will definitely go toward college, because that's something Kristy would have wanted me to do. Kristy always talked about winning the lottery and buying a house on campus. Kristy was always thinking crazy. I can still hear her saying, "Don't worry, Stacy, don't worry."

I have been thinking about Kristy a lot lately. I don't know if I'm going through a new phase in my grieving or what. I have been really sensitive with death. I was watching one of my favorite soap operas and one of Kristy's favorites, and one of the characters had supposedly died, and they were showing the funeral. The next thing I knew, I was crying and couldn't stop. It brought me back to the day of Kristy's funeral. It was like I was experiencing the pain all over again. I had to turn the TV off, because it bothered me too much.

Kristy's birthday was September 15. She would have been twenty years old. That was a very difficult day. I went on a date with Gabe to see to the movie The Glass House. It reminded me so much of Kristy's situation. The main character's parents were killed in a car accident, and she had to live with a couple who just wanted her money from her parents...In the end of the movie it turned out that the couple who she was living with were the ones who killed her parents. The reason it reminded me of Kristy's situation was because Kristy's mom died in a car accident, and her stepmother hated her. Cindy, Kristy's new stepmom, just wanted money from James, not love—money. James was now a rich man with Emily's trust and insurance policy payout. Right now I feel like there should be more for me to do. I should be making sure that Cindy doesn't take James for all of his money. Kristy hated Cindy—with good reason.

Tonight I was out driving with one of my roommates and her friend. We were driving down Como Ave. in St. Paul. We passed A.J.'s Billiards. That was the place that Kristy, Jacob, Jacob's friend Sam, and I went one night the last weekend that we were in Minneapolis. That night was so fun, because Kristy was very good at pool, and I couldn't play whatsoever! Kristy

*was playing against Sam, and she was kicking his ass! It was
so funny, because that was Kristy; she could beat a guy at almost anything if she wanted to. Anyway, tonight we drove past
the billiards place, and it felt like my whole world had stopped.
For about three minutes all I could think about was her and the
times that we had together right before she died. I was sitting in
the backseat of my friend's car, and I just stopped talking. They
noticed something was wrong and asked me why I was being so
quiet. I didn't tell them, because we were having so much fun,
and I didn't want to ruin the moment. The really weird thing
was that at the same time as we were passing A.J.'s Billiards,
an ad on the radio for Sex World came on. When we were in
Minneapolis, Kristy wanted to go to Sex World for some reason—I guess everyone is supposed to go to this so-called store at
least once in her life (well, that's what Kristy said anyway). So
anyway, as I was sitting in the car, it felt like the world around
me just froze in time. I was thinking what it would be like if
Kristy was still alive. I can still picture her driving along, me
in the passenger seat, and she's singing along to a song on the
radio swinging her head, smoking her cigarette, and laughing.*

*I have also decided that Kristy's fight has become my fight.
I can't allow James to acquire a large sum of money from all of
this and have that money end up in the hands of Cindy.*

*This semester has been extremely stressful for me. Not only
am I trying to deal with Kristy's death, but I am also trying to
raise my GPA for my journalism major that I applied for at
the beginning of the semester. I am also very busy with school,
working at Starbucks (which I enjoy greatly!) and Habitat for*

Humanity (*I am the publicity advisor for our U of M Habitat Chapter*). *Also, of course, there are always boy issues. Sometimes I think men are more emotional than women.*

Now that the semester is coming to an end, I realized how hard this semester has been. I don't know if I've really allowed myself to grieve, because I am trying so hard to do well in school and deal with my boyfriend and roommate issues. I am so glad to be done with this semester. I guess it doesn't help that I am taking courses that aren't related to my major but are required for the College of Liberal Arts. Some of my courses are more difficult than I had anticipated. But I'm happy that Christmas is coming. It's going to be hard, though, without Kristy. I remembered how every Christmas we would always call each other up and ask each other what we wanted for Christmas and then call each other up on Christmas and see what we got! So I think it is going to be a bittersweet Christmas. I am so grateful to be alive and to see my family, but on the other hand, I've lost my best friend.

Journal, January 2002

When I got back to my apartment in Minneapolis, I decided to try to find Connor, Kristy's ex-boyfriend, who had some of Kristy's stuff. I knew that Connor had been on probation, so I went on the Internet and found the number for the probation and parole office in Bozeman. I spoke with Connor's parole officer. She informed me that Connor's probation had ended about five or six months before, but she suggested that I call Connor's dad. She said that Connor had planned to go back to Ennis where Kristy lived and had gone to high school for a while. I contacted some of Connor's relatives, and they told me that he wasn't working and had left town. Apparently no one knew where he was. So that pretty much ended my detective streak. ☺

My mom called James's house, because we both wanted to know if he had gotten Kristy's stuff from Connor and to see how he was doing. My mom spoke with a woman named Renee, who is a friend of the family, apparently—even though I'd never heard of her or met her. She told my mom that James had divorced Cindy and was now dating a lady named Gina. Renee also informed my mom that Brent, Kristy's brother, is going into the army in June after he graduates high school.

CHAPTER 13
LEARNING TO DRIVE AGAIN

Journal, August 2003

I've had a fear of driving ever since my first little "accident" with Kristy when we were fifteen years old. That's when Kristy was driving up a steep hill and the Jeep stalled. She couldn't get it under control, and we rolled down the hill into a huge wooden post. The glass broke, and I remember how it shook me up. Then we had the accident in Minneapolis when a kid drove through a red light and we hit him. But after that accident I was able to still drive to work. I seemed to have been working through my fear at that point, plus I was driving a lot. But since this last accident, it seemed to get really bad. My first time driving after the accident, I was driving to work in Sioux Falls and someone cut me off and almost hit me. He would have hit

me, but I slammed on my brakes. I was so upset that I was shak-
ing for the next hour. After that, I didn't drive much. Then I
went back to school in the fall. I don't have a car, so when I'm
at school I don't drive at all. Unless I am backing up one of
my roommates' cars. (We have one lane to park in behind my
apartment building, so when there are three cars back there, we
have to move each car to get out.) That is even difficult for me.
I will sit in the driver's seat, and before I even turn the car on,
my heart starts to race and I tense up...I'm probably in the car
no more than five minutes!

As my journal entry states, after the initial Jeep incident, I became a little fearful of driving. I was fifteen years old and suddenly didn't have a strong interest in driving. My mom told me that I needed to get my license so I could drive myself to school. I made it through getting my license and slowly started to get comfortable driving.

When I went to college, I didn't have a car and didn't need one. I was in Minneapolis, and the transportation system was great. If I didn't want to walk all the way to campus, I could just hop on the campus bus. There wasn't a real need for me to drive, and I liked it that way, especially since I wasn't used to driving in a large city.

The car accident happened the summer before my sophomore year. I was in the passenger seat, so you would think that I would have a fear of being in the passenger seat while someone else drove. But that wasn't the case.

Instead, I had a huge fear of driving myself. Just sitting in the driver's seat, my heart would start racing and my palms would sweat. It was a horribly overwhelming feeling. But I ignored it. I just avoided driving, and it was fine.

The summer of my junior year, I flew out to Seattle to visit my cousin. His wife and daughter were planning on driving to South Dakota to spend a few weeks with our family. So the plan was to ride back to South Dakota with them and then hitch a ride back up to Minneapolis later.

The trip from Seattle to South Dakota is a long drive. It's a beautiful drive, but a long one. I started to feel bad that my cousin's wife was doing all of the driving. She would continually ask me if I wanted to drive, and I continued to say no. Finally, she said that I needed to drive or we would have to stop and stay the night in a hotel, thus delaying us another day. I told her I would do it. I got into the driver's seat and felt panicked, but I told myself that I could do it. Everybody drives, for goodness' sake. I told myself that I was fully capable of driving. Then I thought that perhaps the longer I drove, the more comfortable I would get. That was wishful thinking. I drove for four hours. Once I got out of the car, I realized how tense I was. My entire back hurt, my arms were sore, and I had a headache. It suddenly occurred to me that perhaps I really did have a problem with driving. I knew this wasn't normal, and I asked myself if I really thought that I could live the rest of my life never driving. *Is that even possible? Do I expect to live some rich life where I have a chauffeur who drives me around? That's not realistic.*

So when I got home, I told my mom about my experience and that maybe I needed therapy to get over my fear of driving.

Luckily, on campus there was a therapist who specialized in post-traumatic stress disorder (PTSD). During my first session, she asked me why I was there and what I wanted help with. I told her about the car accident, Kristy, and how I was struggling to drive. She asked me to describe how I felt when I was driving. I told her that I was just so uncomfortable when I drove and I was frustrated that it was such a difficult task. I told her that obviously something wasn't right and that I wanted to get to the point where I could drive like a normal person. I told her that my heart would race, my palms would get sweaty, and I would tense up to the point that my whole body was rigid. She explained to me that those symptoms were very common with PTSD. She said that most people who have been in the passenger seat in a car accident usually suffer from a fear of driving. It's about a loss of control. I had no control over the boy driving the tractor that hit us. I had no control over saving Kristy. I had no control of the van. And therefore, I had no control of my life and was living in fear.

During my sessions, we tried several different tactics. First, she tried pressure points. "Close your eyes and picture yourself in the driver's seat of a car," she said. Then she would tap certain pressure points on my body—mainly my wrists. I would then try tapping myself in the pressure areas, the ones where you would check your pulse or feel your heartbeat: my wrists, my chest over my heart, my neck. It wasn't working. She had me do practice runs. I would sit in my roommate's Jeep in the driver's seat all by myself. I wouldn't have to start the car, just sit in the driver's seat. Then I would write down what I was feeling. Panic. My heart was still racing. I took deep breaths and tried the tapping exercises. It didn't work.

When we weren't making much progress, she hypnotized me. I lay down, made sure I was comfortable, and closed my eyes. She told me that I was going down the steps, deeper and deeper. Then I was sitting on a soft pillow. I was comfortable and safe. Then a steering wheel was in front in me, and a gas pedal and a brake. I would just play in my mind that these objects were safe and fun and picture myself in control.

We did a few of these hypnosis sessions, and I believe they helped me. I started to feel less and less panic each time I got into the driver's seat. I told myself that I could do it and that I needed to be patient with myself and with my mind. I had to make sure that I was in control. I would get in the car and say aloud, "I'm in control, car. Not you. Me." Then I would grip the steering wheel, and when I put my foot on the gas, I reminded myself that I was in control. I only drove short distances at first. I had to pace myself. I drove farther and farther, and it started to get easier.

The true breakthrough was when I got my own car. My very own car! I bought a 2001 VW Passat, a gold four-door sedan. I named her "Goldie." Goldie got me through my tough times. I would talk to her as well, especially when I was driving through any kind of bad weather. She got me from point A to point B safely, every time. Of course, I believe that Kristy was often with me in the car. I would turn the music up loud and sing, just like she used to do when we would go on long car trips.

CHAPTER 14
THE CURSE CONTINUES

I t was my senior year of college, and I was busy taking a full load of credits, working part time at Starbucks, and working part time as a PR intern at a hospital. I was paving my way for the future.

I was still dealing with the aftermath of Kristy's death and the car accident. James had planned to sue the little boy's family, mainly because he was grieving and wanted to take it out on someone. At least that was my perspective on the situation. I didn't agree with James suing the family because I thought it would just continue to open the wounds rather than provide relief. It was an accident. It was God's will. It was what it was, and nothing was going to bring Kristy back. I had accepted that. I hoped that James would do the same. So when James decided to sue the family, I knew that I would be called to the stand to testify. It was going to be a week-long process. I had to ask all of my professors for time away from class and had to explain the situation to them. I had to take some exams outside of class because I was going to miss a week. For weeks I prepped with my lawyer and went over what I was going to say in my head. It was a stressful time. My attorney told me that the family was going to offer James a settlement amount, and if he were to take it, there would be no trial.

The night before the trial, James decided to accept the settlement, which meant there would be no trial. Since I had taken time off of class, I decided to use it as a vacation and stay with my parents. I used the time to reflect on the accident and on Kristy. It was an emotional time. Grieving Kristy's death was a very long, difficult, tedious process.

In May I was gearing up for finals week and graduation. My mom called with some bad news. It was about James. Apparently, his truck went off the road and ran into a tree. He died. Mom heard about it through a mutual family friend. She speculated that it could have been a suicide, because the road conditions were good in Montana at the time. Whether it was an accident or suicide, it was downright eerie. Emily had died in a car accident, and then Kristy died in a car accident, and now James had as well. It was as if their family was cursed. The only living family member was now Brent. If I were him, I would be terrified to drive!

I debated whether to attend James's funeral. I realized that I was still very angry with him, for how he treated Kristy and for his poor decisions after Emily died; I was angry that he cheated on Emily; I was angry that his way of dealing with things was to sue people. I was just angry. It's a difficult thing being angry with someone who is now dead. There's no real closure. A part of me wanted to attend his funeral on behalf of Kristy and Emily. After all, I was very much a part of their family. I had been dragged into their family drama because I felt responsible for Kristy for so many years. Ultimately, I decided not to attend the funeral because it was finals week. My mom reminded me that I was in college for my future, and these were my last finals before graduation. My education should be my top priority.

By not attending the funeral, I don't feel that I ever received full closure on James's death. Sometimes I would forget that he had died. I lost track of Brent, but I often thought of him. I'm not sure how I would deal with my entire family being dead, with being the only one left at such a young age. From what I heard, he went into the military and is now married and has a few children. Knowing that he has made a good life for himself brings me peace.

CHAPTER 15

LOVE LIFE

As I look back, I realize Kristy taught me so much about life. She taught me to stand up for myself, to live my own life, to take risks, and to believe in myself. She also taught me not to take things too seriously and not to worry; things eventually work out the way they are supposed to. See, each one of us is on a path or a journey through life. I believe that God does have a plan for each one of us. I think that society sometimes forgets that. We expect everyone to follow the same the path, and that's not right, especially when it comes to women. We should embrace our different paths, help one another, encourage one another, and build each other up. Too often I see jealous women who try to break down other women or say bad things about them. This happens not only in the workplace but in our personal lives as well. My hope is that members of the next generation of women learn to support, encourage, and build up one another.

I guess my track record with men wasn't always the best. After Kristy died, I felt such emptiness in my heart. It was like a gaping hole that needed to be filled. I could have turned to drugs, alcohol, or food or started risky behaviors or hobbies, but instead I wanted love. Feeling loved was the only way to make that emptiness go away. I was still sort of seeing my boyfriend from high school, but then in college I started a relationship with another man, and then a third one came along. It's not that I didn't care about them; I cared very much for all of them, so much so that I didn't want to let any of them go. So I did the selfish thing and kept seeing all three of them for several months. They didn't know about each other, so I just kept the all of the relationships going because I felt loved. I knew at the time that what I was doing was wrong; I just didn't want to hurt anyone or feel loss. I had enough loss with Kristy's death.

After a few months and a few close calls of the guys finding out about each other, I knew I needed to stop the first two relationships. I started to fall hard for the third guy. Something about him made me think that he was "The One." Looking back now, I really have no idea why I loved him. He was athletic, business-minded, and came from a good family. Little did I know he would break my heart into a million pieces.

After I broke things off with the first two guys, I almost lost the third one. He said he wasn't sure about me. We dated through college and continued seeing each other after we both graduated. We were in a relationship for a total of four and a half years.

Gabe was a happy-go-lucky guy, and he made me happy when I was with him. He lived in Iowa, so we had a long-distance relationship. I treasured our time together, because it was often a day here or there. I called him every morning on my way to work. He owned his own landscaping company, so he could take my calls in the morning while he was outside working.

My friends didn't like Gabe. Something about him and the way he treated me just didn't sit right with them. (I guess they caught on way before I did.) I considered moving to his hometown to be with him. At the time we discussed this, he told me I could move to Iowa in six months. Even though we had dated for over four years, I had never met his parents. We had never celebrated holidays together, nor had we ever gone on a vacation together. He had never said, "I love you." My mom, being very protective of me, felt something wasn't right. So she called Gabe's parents one day without telling me. As it turned out, they didn't know anything about me. They told my mom that Gabe had been dating his high school sweetheart for many years and that she was pregnant with his child. In fact, they were considering buying a house together. Furious, my mom told his parents that Gabe had one week to break things off with me—or else.

The week came and went, and Gabe didn't say anything to me. My mom called and said she was coming to Minneapolis for the weekend and that she had a surprise for me. When she picked me up, she started driving south to Iowa. I asked her where we were going and what we were doing. She explained her phone conversation with Gabe's parents. I couldn't believe it. I was in complete and utter shock. I wanted to throw up and cry at the same time. It was as if someone had ripped my heart from my chest and then stomped on it. My mind started racing. Who was this woman from his high school? Ah, yes, it was Hannah. Gabe had told me about her. They had dated all through high school and now were good friends. She called him sometimes to give him updates on their hometown high school football games. *He lied to me. He was seeing her the whole time we've been together. That bastard!* I had never felt so used in my entire life.

When we got to Gabe's hometown, we found his parents. They felt bad about what Gabe had done to me and said they'd talk with him. Gabe was out of town; how convenient for him. I called him and told him that we were finished. I told him that I wished him much happiness with Hannah. Then my mom drove me back to Minneapolis.

I took a week off of work and went home to my parents' house, where I got little sleep and cried for days. I was a wreck. This was a totally different kind of loss. I was heartbroken, hurt, ashamed, embarrassed, and at the same time, angry. Then the anger would go away, because I still loved him.

I learned that love isn't a switch that can just be turned off. It takes time for our hearts and minds to understand that someone doesn't love us back. It takes time for our hearts to stop harboring those loving feelings. For me, it created fear—love makes us vulnerable. The fear of getting hurt—feeling heartbroken again— was a devastating thought.

As I was grappling with heartbreak and starting to pick myself up, I sent Gabe a text asking him to get rid of anything personal that he had of mine. A few moments later, my phone rang. It was Gabe's number.

"Hello," I said.

"Hi. What do you think you are doing with my boyfriend?" said a female voice.

"Is this Hannah?"

"Yes. Stay away from my man, bitch," Hannah responded.

"I want nothing to do with your man. I didn't know anything about you until about two weeks ago. I broke things off with him. I never would have continued to see him if I had known he was with you. I'm sorry," I responded.

"Well, okay then. Stop texting him," Hannah said more calmly.

"No problem," I said.

I ended the call, thinking it was a damn good thing it was over with Gabe. Then I started to wonder why. How could he have lied to me all these years? What was he doing with me anyway? Why hadn't he just ended things with me? Now he was going to be a dad and a husband—with some other woman, not me. My life that I pictured with him—my future that I felt so strongly about—was all a big fat lie. He had used me. I was his secret girlfriend, his lover. The other woman. I felt like a dirty whore, ashamed and totally embarrassed that I would get myself into a fake relationship and allow myself to be used.

When this all went down, it was before the big push of social media. I wasn't using Facebook yet, but if I had been on it, he would have been in big trouble.

A few months passed, and I was still struggling to get over Gabe. Early on, I would dream about him and then wake up and realize we weren't together. My heart ached. I'd get a lump in my throat and catch myself before I started to cry. I was on the verge of forgiving him. I loved him so much that I was willing to overlook his mistakes. Perhaps our love was only meant to last four years, and his future was with Hannah.

One day, out of the blue, Hannah called me again. She was seven months pregnant.

"Hi, Stacy. It's Hannah."

"How's it going?" I replied.

"Well, I felt like I needed to call and tell you the whole story," said Hannah.

"Okay," I said fearfully.

"You aren't the only other woman…" she began.

"*What?* What do you mean?" I replied, shocked and feeling like I was going to throw up.

"Gabe had been hiding his phone from me. I thought it was weird that he kept charging it in his truck. Something just didn't seem right," Hannah said. "So when he was in the shower, I went out to his truck and started looking through his phone. He made up male names for the women in his phone. You're listed as 'David.'"

I realized that I had never looked at his phone and never noticed that my name wasn't in it.

"The other woman lives in Tennessee, and I actually met her!" Hannah explained.

"Go on," I said.

"Oh my God, her name is Natalie—she's old, like forty And she's ugly! She has no class whatsoever!" Hannah said.

I was chuckling inside a bit. "What did you say to her?"

"That Gabe was with me. He got me pregnant, and we are getting married," she said. "The dumb bitch doesn't believe me! Then I told her about you—that you live in Minneapolis. She doesn't believe that you exist either. She thinks I'm making this up because I'm still in love with Gabe. I got to thinking that you really had no idea about all of this, and that you are just as much a victim as I am."

"Well, that is true. I'm sorry, I'm just in shock that he was seeing another woman in addition to both of us," I said as my stomach did a flip.

"Yeah, well, I'm thinking of breaking things off with Gabe. He's lied to me, and I don't just have myself to think about anymore. I have a baby on the way, and I need to think about his or her life as well," she said firmly. "The thing is, I don't know how many other women there are. I know there are more than three. I've just figured out about you and dumb Natalie."

Then her tone changed, and I could sense she still didn't fully trust me.

"I think that's enough for now," she said. "Would it be okay if I called you again?"

"Absolutely. Again, I'm really sorry all of this happened. Thanks for letting me know about Natalie. I'm in shock. Let me know if there is anything I can do," I replied. I thought that I was the lucky one in this situation. I wasn't pregnant. I didn't live near him, and I didn't have to see him every day. I sobbed and sobbed. I cried out of confusion, loss, heartache, and pain—pain for myself, pain for Hannah, and pain for her and Gabe's unborn child.

As the days went on, a million things were going through my head. I wasn't the "other woman." I wasn't sure who I was to Gabe. I wasn't sure what our relationship meant to him. I have no idea who this man is/was…It was the weirdest feeling in the world. Then I got angry.

This was all just a game to him. Some sick, twisted, fucked-up game. *Who does this? What kind of person does this to women? How could he do this? And with a child involved?* Unforgiveable. I didn't know who this man was. He was certainly not the man I fell in love with. I really didn't know who Gabe was—at all. Maybe he had multiple personalities. That must be it. A normal, functioning person could not do something like this. *And for years!* He was sick. Sick in his head. I'd be damned if I was going to let him get away with this. He needed to be taught a lesson.

As if he could hear me, the next thing I knew, I received a text message from Gabe. *Wow, this is something you'd see on a Jerry Springer show. Un-freaking-believable.*

The text from Gabe said, "Can we talk? I miss you." *Crap! What should I do?* I thought.

I decided to text Hannah. I told her that Gabe wanted to talk to me, and I wasn't sure how I should respond to him. Hannah replied that I should talk to him.

I gathered my strength and replied to his text. "Sure, we can talk." My phone rang.

"Hi," I said calmly.

"Hey, what's up?" Gabe asked.

"Not a whole lot. But I do have a question for you," I said, straight-faced.

"Sure," said Gabe.

"What the hell were you thinking? You were screwing another woman besides me and Hannah?" I yelled.

"I don't know what you are talking about or how you would even know," he replied.

"I have my ways. You disgust me. I don't even know who you are," I said sadly.

"Well, I don't know where you got this information, but it's not true," he said. A part of me wanted to believe him—that this whole thing was some kind of misunderstanding. Then I caught myself and got a grip. *God, he's seriously going to deny this and lie to me some more? I need to be smart about this.*

"So you are telling me that you haven't been screwing some woman in Tennessee?"

"No," he said.

"Okay, well, whatever. What did you want to talk to me about?"

"Just that I miss you and want to see you again," he said.

"Well, that's not going to happen any time soon. I need some time to calm down," I told him.

"Can I call you again?" he asked.

"Sure," I replied, thinking it might be good to still stay in touch with him.

I started to get smart about everything. I figured I needed to stay at least one step ahead of Gabe. I could have chosen to just stay out of everything, but the reality was that I was in this triangle of a mess—Hannah and the baby, me, and this other woman. It wasn't right. He shouldn't be allowed to get away with this. To hurt people like this. To treat women like this. No, I wasn't going to let him get away with it.

I avoided calling Gabe or taking his calls. Instead, I would text or e-mail him so that there was a record of what he said. That way, it was easy to forward any texts or e-mails to Hannah or anyone else.

After the baby was born, Hannah began the legal process to make sure that Gabe didn't get full custody. I told her that I was more than willing to help in any way that I could. I didn't believe that Gabe was capable of being a good father. How can a man be a good father when he is bringing random women home to screw? The man was obviously preoccupied with his penis. *He doesn't even deserve a penis.* A man like that is not capable of being a good father, and quite frankly, he doesn't deserve to be a father at all.

I sent Hannah all of my correspondence with Gabe. Often he would say things like, "I'm not with Hannah and have no interest in having a life with her and the baby." He even created a video pleading with me to take him back. He was doing everything he could to make sure that I thought he was only thinking about me. Then, of course, he would turn around and say the same things to Hannah. The correspondence came in handy because it was very clear Gabe was a pathological liar, and some might even classify him has having some kind of mental illness.

At some point he found out I was sending Hannah all of our messages. He was furious.

"Why don't you just stay out of my business?" he yelled over the phone.

"You made it my fucking business when you decided to screw Hannah while you were with me!" I yelled back.

"I can't believe you would do something like this. I guess now I know the real you," he said angrily.

"Yeah, well, I'm still trying to figure out who the hell you are. I thought I knew who I was dating for four years, and then I find out you've been sleeping with a bunch of other women!" I said.

"I think we are done talking," Gabe responded.

"Yeah, I guess we are," I replied.

After that, I didn't hear much from Gabe. Until Valentine's Day. I was working for a major PR agency, and my mother sent me flowers. It was so sweet of her. An hour later, I received an embarrassing amount of roses. Boxes and boxes of pink roses. It took me twenty minutes to open all of them. I started to count them. There were a hundred pink roses. I couldn't believe it.

I didn't know what to do. Should I throw them away? But I *love* pink roses. It wasn't the roses' fault that Gabe was a complete asshole. I asked my coworkers what they would do in my shoes (those who knew what had happened). One person suggested that I let the roses die and send them back to him. I found a vase large enough to hold all of them and put them on my desk while I decided what to do. People started talking about my roses. The president even stopped by my desk to see them! Finally, I decided I should enjoy them. After everything he put me through, I deserved them. I would look at these roses and not think of him. I also decided that I certainly didn't need a hundred pink roses, and there were plenty of other single women in my office who didn't receive any flowers on Valentine's Day, so I decided to walk around handing them out. It was a great feeling!

Dealing with heartbreak is a long process, much like grieving the death of a loved one. There's shock, disbelief, denial, anger, sadness, and finally acceptance. I think the longer you are with someone, the longer the "grieving" process will be. After my shock, disbelief, and denial phase was done, anger filled me. But it wasn't just anger that I was dealing with; I was also dealing with betrayal. Years of betrayal. My anger didn't stop just at Gabe, either. I became angry with most men. I didn't trust them anymore. I didn't want men to touch me. If a man was nice to me, I just thought he was out to use me. I thought that all that men wanted was sex—to use me for sex and then leave. I dealt with this anger for years. It took me almost four years to work through my anger and to be open to men and love again.

CHAPTER 16

YOUNG PROFESSIONAL

From 2005 to 2009, I worked in Minneapolis for one of the world's largest PR agencies. It was a fantastic job opportunity, and I had started as an intern. It was my first real job in my field. I moved up the ladder and eventually became an account executive. I learned many things during my time at the agency: my writing skills were not superior; everything must be proofed, no matter what your position; you are never done learning; strong leaders know they get ahead because of solid teamwork; work is much more enjoyable when you make friends there; always go above and beyond; time management is crucial; everyone makes mistakes, and it's okay to admit when you've made one; and know your worth.

I worked on several client accounts and excelled at doing media relations. I really enjoyed my job but learned how quickly you can get burned out. Agency work is fast-paced and competitive. You are never really off the clock, and you don't work from eight to five.

Around 2008 the economy started to take a downturn. A big downturn. It was the recession, and I remember colleagues and experts talking about the negative impact it was going to have on our clients, on our agency, on our city, on our state, and on our country. But what really hit home was people were losing their jobs. I wasn't in a very good position—we had lost my main client, not because of wrongdoing on our part, but simply because the client had a change in leadership and was looking for ways to decrease costs. It was a terrifying time. People were slowly being let go. Then it happened to me.

Before this happened, there was a shift inside of me. I'm not sure what brought it on, but I had been thinking of moving back to South Dakota to be closer to my family. I started looking for jobs there, but with no luck. Then, when I lost my job with the PR agency, I had no choice but to move back. With no job, I couldn't pay my rent. I was able to get a friend to sublease the apartment, and my brother and now sister-in-law let me live with them in Sioux Falls.

So there I was. No job. No boyfriend. No place of my own. Being let go leaves you with a feeling that you weren't good enough to keep around. It was a very depressing time for me. I was asking myself why I was here and what my purpose was. I kept thinking that maybe I should have been the one to die, and not Kristy. I thought that perhaps she would have done more with her life in her twenties than I had.

I did have plenty of things to be thankful for: I had a nice place to live and was surrounded by family; I was in good health; I was receiving unemployment compensation; and I had lots of free time! So, after feeling sorry for myself, I decided that I needed to pick myself up, put on my big-girl pants, and make the most of my situation.

My grandmother was living in Sioux Falls, so I took this opportunity to spend time with her every single day. I helped with various things like going shopping for her, taking her to doctor's appointments, and just being there with her. I spent a lot of time at the retirement center where she lived, and I got to know a lot of wonderful people.

But I didn't stop there. I knew I needed to keep my skills up, so I volunteered with Habitat for Humanity in Sioux Falls on their PR committee and helped plan a big fundraising event for Habitat for Humanity South Dakota. I joined a young professionals group and met some of my closest friends. I ended up with a very busy lifestyle. I went out almost every chance I got. I worked out every single day and was in the best shape of my life. One of the best takeaways I had from being unemployed is that I learned that my career does not define who I am.

I was unemployed for about nine months. Through the friendships I had developed, I got a job doing investor relations for a private company in Sioux Falls. It was a drastic change from the agency, a strict eight-to-five job with only men in company leadership positions. It was a red flag to me working for a company where only men made the final business decisions. There were times where I felt I was degraded because I was a woman. I learned a lot at that job, including that it wasn't for me.

During that time, I met my boyfriend, Ben, who lived in Brookings. Our relationship continued to grow, and it was only a matter of time before one of us needed to move.

Since Ben held a good position and owned his own house, I knew I needed to make the change and make the move. I accepted a marketing position in Brookings.

I'll admit it was a scary thing to move to a smaller community where I didn't really know anyone except for Ben and some of his friends.

I refused to move in with Ben until we were engaged, so I lived in an apartment until the ring came. During that time, I became involved with various planning committees, participated in Leadership Brookings, and made every effort possible to meet new people and make new friends. Turns out, Brookings is an amazing community to live in!

CHAPTER 17

LOVE, MARRIAGE, AND CHILDREN

What is it about love that makes people go crazy? Maybe it's not so much love, but marriage. When you are younger, people think you need to get married and have children. When you hit thirty and aren't married and don't have children, people suddenly start wondering what's wrong with you. I was in a relationship with my boyfriend when I was thirty, but we weren't engaged yet. People always seemed to judge our relationship. *Is he is going to marry you? What if he doesn't—then you are wasting your life with this man, and you are in your thirties. You don't have time to waste if you want kids.*

I'm so thankful I didn't get married or have children in my twenties. I believe those years are meant to focus on finding yourself, discovering what you want in life, and advancing your career. It's astonishing to look at numerous studies that show that people who marry after the age twenty-five are much less likely to get divorced; after age thirty, the rate of divorce dramatically decreases.

I love my boyfriend more than anything; he is a wonderful, amazing man. The problem is, he doesn't express his emotions. He's a private man who doesn't share his feelings with friends and family. When we were dating, many people weren't sure if he really loved me, or if he was serious about me. I could tell that his family was used to him bringing women home and not having lasting relationships. Ben wasn't "googly-eyed" or gushing in love; that just isn't his personality. So when we did get engaged, a lot of people were shocked. I should point out that Ben was thirty-nine years old and I was thirty-one. I think some people thought he would never get married since he was pushing forty. Apparently, our society thinks that if a man isn't married by the time he is thirty-five, he will never marry.

Ben wasn't divorced, nor had he ever been engaged. In his defense, he worked overseas for six years in his early thirties, a time when most men in the United States get married. He wasn't ready to get married (and, of course, he hadn't met me). Our relationship was never perfect—no relationship is—but I knew that he was the one for me, and eventually he would get to the point where he was ready to marry me. Ben never had a commitment problem. I believe he had a fear of divorce, which was perhaps why he rarely talked about marriage to his friends and family.

Our closest friends watched Ben change, transform, and grow. I believe that when you are with the right partner, you grow together and grow as individuals. You bring out the best in each other. Our love, and my patience and persistence, helped him come out of his shell and open his heart to let me in. It was almost magical, like a caterpillar growing into a butterfly.

It was a relief when he proposed. It's hard as a woman, always wondering and worrying if he will ever marry you. He always told me that he wanted to be with me, that I didn't have to worry, but I also always told him that I wanted to get married. I made that very clear early on when we started dating. To be exact, I told him that I'd give a man two years. If he didn't propose within that time, I'd walk away from the relationship because I was not a woman who would wait around for a man to make up his damn mind. I was worthy, and I deserved to be with a man who loved me and wanted to share his life with me.

So when Ben proposed, it was like a big weight was lifted off my shoulders. I didn't have to worry anymore. I had a permanent smile on my face. It wasn't about the ring or about the upcoming wedding; it was about the two of us sharing the rest of our lives and making that commitment to solidify our love. We'd been together for three and a half years, so we had certainly had our ups and downs. Getting engaged was like winning the race—all of the hurdles and obstacles, as well as all of the good times, were worth it. It's sort of like closing the book on one chapter of your life—or rather a big, long, young chapter and opening the next chapter of the rest of your life. But the best part is you have a partner next to you, taking your hand to be by your side through the challenging, difficult times and through the fun, loving, wonderful, amazing times.

I'm not saying that every woman has to get married. There are plenty of women who walk through life without a husband. Their partner may be a close friend or a relative, for example. And they will have wonderful and fulfilling lives. I have often heard the phrase "When you get married..." How do these people know that I want to get married? It's one of the worst things to say to a single woman. Respect her singlehood.

But I do think that there is something special and divine about having a true partner who loves you completely and stands by your side.

I worry about young couples—those who marry in their early twenties—because I don't think they've had enough life experience to get through marriage. I think it is more difficult in your early twenties. Perhaps we will always change over time, but in my thirties, I can confidently say that I know who I am, and I know what I want. In your twenties, you are still trying to figure out those things. I think when you put marriage into that mix, a lot of couples don't make it. It's a rare couple who marries young, stays married, and is actually happy. However, I can say that I have several friends who fit into that category. Not many people can say that. Bottom line, everyone is different, but I think as a society, we shouldn't push young people to get married. We need to allow young men and women the space to determine what their path is.

I hope in the many years ahead that I will be able to say that Ben and I are still in love and are happy together. I realize that marriage takes work. It doesn't magically happen that way. Happy couples know that marriage takes work and that you have to make your partner a priority.

I find it interesting that most women will say something like this: "When you have children..." Why do they assume that (1) I want to have children and (2) that I'm able to have children? Why does our society make those assumptions? How hurtful would it be to say that to a woman who is unable to have children? And even if she can have children, maybe she doesn't want to have them—not every woman *wants* that. I've also heard the phrase "We weren't blessed with children." I'm not entirely sure what this means. Does it mean that the couple wasn't able to have children? Even so, adoption is an option. Instead, I often think that the couple just decided not to have children, and because they feel societal pressures that everyone should have children, they've come up with that phrase.

I'm still not sure if I want children. I worry about it. I worry that children will take too much of my time—that I will put too much of myself into my children and not into my spouse. The last thing I want is to be unhappy. For years, I've watched friends and family get married and have children. One thing I've observed is that people absolutely love their children, but sometimes they neglect their spouse. They neglect their relationships; they are exhausted; they let themselves go; they put dreams on hold; they put vacations on hold.

There are also plenty of people who don't do these things. They have figured out how to properly balance work, children, friendships, and time with their spouse. I'm sure it's not easy, though. Some people put their children last on their list. And I don't believe that is right, either. Call me selfish, but I love my life! I have the freedom to change jobs if I want. We have the freedom to go on a two- or three-week vacations across the world. We have the freedom to sleep in or wake up early and enjoy pure quiet. We have the freedom to sit outside on a warm summer evening having a glass of wine or a beer without interruptions. Ben has the freedom to travel weeks on end for his job—and he can come home knowing that I'm fine. If we had children and he was gone for two weeks, he would probably come home to me handing him the kids as I walk out the door for some peace and quiet or time with my friends. I'm afraid to give up this freedom. I'm also still waiting for this so-called "urge" to have children. Perhaps after we get married, it may surface.

Kids are a lot of work, time, effort, and money. Yes, you have this human being that you created and experience this love like no other (this information is all based on other people's experience), but people with young kids always seem to be giving up a lot. It's the lucky people who have nannies and cleaning people, and their lives are a little easier. The problem is most people can't afford those services. I guess if you make sacrifices to have children, you do so because you really want to have children. I do believe that children are precious, wonderful gifts from God. I think some women's life purposes are to be mothers. They dedicate their lives to raising their children and they lead happy, fulfilling lives.

I've been warned that once we get married, we will be flooded with questions about having children. *When are you going to have children? How many children will you have?* I have a friend who went through this scenario. She was my age, and she and her partner did want kids, but she had medical issues that were preventing her from having children. She went through surgeries. She had two miscarriages. They fought a private battle, and it broke my heart to hear her talk about her struggles and how insensitive people can be. Luckily for my friend, she was finally able to give birth to a beautiful baby girl.

It's none of your business if a couple wants or doesn't want to have children. It's none of your business how many children a couple wants. It's none of your business if a couple wants to adopt. We need to be more respectful of people's choices.

What I've found most interesting is that I'm beginning to have real conversations with people about children. Mothers with young children have started to talk about the reality of kids—that they are exhausted and don't get much sleep. Full-time working mothers say that spending more than three days with their kids is all they can take.

"Kids are so much work."

"We love our kids, but it's really hard to balance everything."

"Seriously consider whether you want to have kids."

I've also noticed how important it is for mothers to have support from other mothers. I'm talking about nonjudgmental support. From what I've seen, it's hard being a mom. It's even more difficult if other mothers are judging how you parent. Breastfeed or formula? Cosleeping? Stay-at-home mom, full time working mom, or part time working mom? Daycare or nanny? Spank or no discipline? Preschool? There are a lot of pressures to being a mother, and I'm sure I've only touched on a few areas. From what I've seen, first-time mothers are stressed about making the right decisions when it comes to parenting, but when I see first-time mothers open up honestly about issues they are having, the support from other mothers seems to really help them. I think sometimes all we need is reassurance that what we are doing is okay.

It has me thinking about what I heard author Elizabeth Gilbert say about women: There are three categories: (1) women who are born to be mothers; (2) women who are born to be aunties; and (3) women who should not be near children. Not every woman has to be a mother. Do I think I'd be a horrible mother? No, not at all. I think I'd be great. I don't believe in having children for the sake of having them and then focusing purely on one's career. Sure, you can "have it all" or "do it all," and somehow our society seems to pride itself on "doing it all," but at what cost? I feel that if I'm going to have children, I want to be able to dedicate my time to them. I also know that I don't want to be a stay-at-home mom. My ideal situation would be to work part time. I think everyone's situation is different, and we need to make choices that fit our own situations. It's not fair to pigeonhole everyone.

I think back to Kristy's relationship with her mother. Emily worked full time and didn't "baby" or shelter Kristy and Brent. They had farm chores every day and helped clean the house. Emily would sometimes travel for her job; since she was travel agent, she would travel to various locations to check them out. During these travel times, Kristy was responsible for cooking meals for her dad and brother as well as their farm hired man.

Emily was an affectionate, yet stern mother. You didn't want to upset Emily, because she would put you in your place so quickly. I remember Brent got into trouble once because he kept repeating a swear word, so Emily put a bar of soap in his mouth! Needless to say, Brent stopped using that word. Emily didn't care what other parents thought of her; she raised her kids to the best of her ability and managed her family how she pleased.

CHAPTER 18
JULY 3, 2014

Thirteen years ago today, my best friend and I were in a horrific car accident. If you saw pictures of the vehicle, you would look at me in disbelief, amazed that I walked away alive and with no broken bones. I'm a walking miracle. This day always reminds me of how lucky I am. It reminds me not to take things for granted, to appreciate each and every day and everyone in my life. So every day, I must be thankful for my blessings: my fiancé, my family, my friends, my home, my career. Every night before I go to sleep, I look at my fiancé, and I thank God for him. He is the best thing that has happened to me since Kristy.

I am thankful for the things we take for granted on a daily basis, like walking, having all of my limbs, and being able to speak, eat, hear, and smell. I'm reminded that God has a plan for me. I was left here to do something, to be somebody. So what was I left here to do? I'm not entirely sure, but I do know that writing this book is one of those things. Sometimes I think that once we are done doing what we are supposed to do, we die. I have always wondered what Kristy's purpose was...and when she completed that purpose. Was it in Minneapolis on our trip? Did her purpose have something to do with me? I guess I'll never know.

Once a year I go to the crash site. For the first ten years, I always cried and was exhausted. After a decade, the tears stopped. It's as if I've become numb, or perhaps I've finally accepted it for what it is. It's not my doing; it was God's plan. All I can do is my best every day and keep on living. I believe with my whole heart and soul that Kristy is with me. Not every day, but sometimes she is here with me. I talk to her and ask for her help. I see her as my guardian angel. But who knows? Perhaps she is busy helping others as well.

I'm preparing to get married, and I miss Kristy dearly...She was supposed to be my maid of honor. We made that promise to each other a few months before the accident. When I look back, I wonder whether she knew her time here was almost done; she was having dreams about her mom a few months before the accident.

CHAPTER 19
BACHELORETTE PARTY

It's the one special time in every woman's life as she's about to get married: the bachelorette party! My friends organized an amazing day, including all of my favorite things: lots of pink, lots of wine, good friends, and laughter. Being thirty-two years old, I didn't want a traditional bachelorette party involving going to bars. Instead, we went to several wineries! We had a party bus and sang, danced, and even hung from a pole on the ceiling of the bus. Great memories were made. The only thing missing was my best friend, Kristy. It was one of those important moments in life. Sure, I had almost twenty friends with me—there was no shortage of them—but the one person who should have been there was missing. I do know that she was there in spirit, and she helped make sure that I had a good time and that everything went well for me.

Looking at the pictures from that day and evening, I was all smiles. I took pictures with the whole group and with individual friends. But not with Kristy. I wonder what it would have been like if she were still alive, and what her bachelorette party would have been like. I imagine it would have been much different from mine, filled with a different kind of craziness. I imagine male strippers, *lots* of alcohol, and exposed skin. But then again, who knows what Kristy would have been like at thirty-two? She could have calmed down and changed her ways, changed her interests, her likes, and dislikes. You change a lot in your twenties.

It's strange to wonder what she would have been like, what our friendship would have been like, who she would have married, and if she would have kids. Those thoughts are common for anyone who has lost someone close at a young age. There are so many unanswered questions and might-have-beens…but we can't think like that. We have to acknowledge what was and the time that was spent on Earth. It wasn't God's plan to have Kristy live to thirty-two, or even twenty-five. Ask yourself what you were like and who you were at age nineteen. Are you the same today? I highly doubt it. We are constantly growing and changing.

Friendships change as well. At my bachelorette party, I had friends from high school, college, my midtwenties, and early thirties. I had friends from Minneapolis, St. Paul, Sioux Falls, and Brookings. A lot of these ladies stuck with me; many have seen me at my worst. But one thing was certain: I had finally found my happiness with the love of my life. And that deserves celebration! I wasn't saying farewell to singlehood; I felt that I had already said good-bye to that years ago when I started dating Ben. What flashed in my mind was that I was so thankful for him. I didn't feel that I was "losing out on being single" or "being handcuffed to one man for the rest of my life." No, this was a time to celebrate something wonderful. It was also an excuse to have a big, blowout party with friends in a way that only fellow girl-friends could understand and appreciate.

I now feel ready and prepared, and I have realistic expectations for marriage. I know it takes work, and not every day will be sunshine and roses. But I feel equipped to weather the storm, and I'm making a commitment to my love to stay with him until the day we die. If that idea scares you, or if you are uncertain, you are probably not with the right man. When you are with the right person, you know deep inside that it will work for the long haul.

CHAPTER 20

WEDDING

I've made many big, positive decisions in my life: going to college in Minneapolis, making my relationship work with Ben, making the move to Brookings, and having a destination wedding.

Sure, our wedding had some snags, but overall, it was a great decision and the best thing for us.

Planning a wedding is stressful, even when it's a destination wedding. There are a lot of details to iron out and decide on, and then there's the stress of getting everyone to your location! Ben was actively involved in every step of our wedding process, and it made me appreciate him and further solidified my conviction that I was marrying the right man.

We got married in Tulum, Mexico, and it was absolutely beautiful! The ceremony took place on the beach under a wooden canopy with white linen and gorgeous pink and white lilies. Sixty people attended, and we kept everything within our budget. Having a wedding coordinator at the resort helped relieve the stress of dealing with details.

But it wasn't just about the wedding—it was the day when Ben and I made a commitment to one another to stay together through the tough times, and to love and respect each other. It's easy to stay together when things are going well and you are both so happy, but I believe the real test of any relationship is when difficult things arise. I've learned so much about relationships over the eleven months of our engagement. I've learned not to compare our relationship with others'—every couple is different; I've learned to put Ben first, and about the importance of compromise; I've learned that when you give love, you receive it; I've learned that because every couple is different, you have to figure out what makes you happy as a couple and what works for the two of you.

There were several people missing from our wedding, one being my dad, who got sick right before the wedding and wasn't able to travel to Mexico, but also many loved ones who had passed. For me, Kristy wasn't there.

Getting married makes you look back on your life. For me, my journey has had plenty of ups and downs. I have emotional scars that will stay with me forever. Some people come into our lives and make a profound impact. They change our lives forever. For me, Kristy was one of those people. Most of the time, she drove me nuts, always pushing limits and stretching my comfort zones. But I suppose it was good for me. We were polar opposites. I was the Goody Two-shoes, she was the bad apple. Our friendship left a mark on me, much like a fingerprint, engrained in me and on my soul.

I think Kristy would have approved of Ben. Sometimes I wonder if she somehow brought the two of us together. Now that we're married, it really feels like I'm starting a new chapter—together with the love of my life.

Made in the USA
Middletown, DE
12 January 2016